# Under the Table and Into Your Pocket
The How and Why of the Underground Economy

### by Bill Wilson

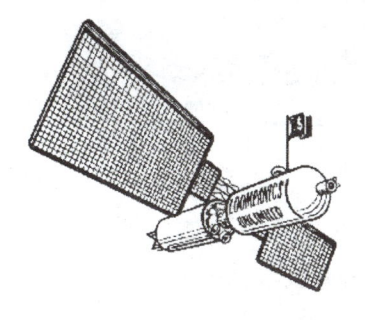

Loompanics Unlimited
Port Townsend, Washington

*Neither the author nor the publisher assumes any responsibility for the use or misuse of information contained in this book. It is sold for informational purposes only. Be Warned!*

## Under the Table and Into Your Pocket
### The How and Why of the Underground Economy
© 2005 by Bill Wilson

All rights reserved. No part of this book may be reproduced or stored in any form whatsoever without the prior written consent of the publisher. Reviews may quote brief passages without the written consent of the publisher as long as proper credit is given.

**Published by:**
Loompanics Unlimited
PO Box 1197
Port Townsend, WA 98368
Loompanics Unlimited is a division of Loompanics Enterprises, Inc.
Phone: 360-385-2230
Fax: 360-385-7785
E-mail: service@loompanics.com
Web site: www.loompanics.com

Cover art: L.S. Willilams, Jr.

**ISBN 1-55950-243-6**
**Library of Congress Card Catalog Number 2005921855**

# Contents

Introduction ............................................................. 1

**Chapter One**
Foundations of a Free Economy ........................... 3

**Chapter Two**
Taxes, Licenses, Monopolies. Oh, my! ................ 9

**Chapter Three**
Feeding the Tax Monster ..................................... 21

**Chapter Four**
The Buck Starts Here ........................................... 31

**Chapter Five**
Case Histories ....................................................... 53

**Chapter Six**
Red Light Work .................................................. 101

**Appendix:**
How to Make Money from Storage
    Building Auctions ........................................... 107
Works Cited/Resources for Further Study ........ 113

# INTRODUCTION

This is a book about the underground economy. First and foremost it is about freedom — the freedom to choose one's destiny, to develop skills, acquire goods and trade freely and honestly with others. These freedoms, guaranteed by the United States Constitution, have been bought with the blood of countless patriots over the last two centuries, and are still worth fighting for.

The primary enemy is a centralized government with a never-ending lust for both power and money — our money. It might be said that the Revolutionary War is still being fought. But now the bullets are dollars, and the opposing army is the IRS, which along with corrupt politicians at every level, seeks to crush the flame of economic liberty.

This is also a book about heroes, men and women who refuse to kowtow meekly before an oppressive foe. Like their forefathers, they struggle valiantly and against great odds to exercise the most basic rights they have. They do so not out of a spirit of malice or selfishness, but from a simple conviction that what they work for is theirs by right, and that no one should be allowed to pick their pockets.

Finally, it is a book about opportunity — opportunity to make a good living anywhere in the United States, with one's brain and muscle. Such opportunities still exist, despite layer upon layer of regulations that tell us what to do, where to go, and what to think. America is quickly becoming a totalitarian nanny state, but in the midst of it all there is still the chance to make a buck.

It has been a moving experience to write these words, and I want to thank the good folks at Loompanics for giving me the chance to do so. I also want to acknowledge my wonderful wife, who has been tirelessly supportive and encouraging. Most of all I give thanks to God, from whom all human freedoms flow. I trust that you will find this book both illuminating and inspiring, and I thank you as well for reading it. Best wishes to you all.

Bill Wilson<br>
February 2005

# Chapter One
# Foundations of A Free Economy

*"A wise and frugal government, which shall leave men free to regulate their own pursuits of industry and improvement, and shall not take from their mouths the bread they have earned — this is the sum of good government."* — Thomas Jefferson

### Traditional American Democracy

On August 2, 1776, fifty-six men gathered in Philadelphia, Pennsylvania, to sign the Declaration of Independence. It had been formally adopted by the Continental Congress almost a month earlier, but the actual signing was delayed until it had been approved by each state. By affixing their signatures, each of the men was putting his very life at risk, defying the most powerful force on earth at that time, the British Empire.

Embodied in the Declaration are the philosophical foundations of both representative democracy and capitalism. It contains the ideas which govern the most free and prosperous society ever to exist. These ideas were further developed in its sister document, the Constitution.

The concepts within those two documents have been under assault for more than two centuries, by those who prefer to see men as slaves rather than free individuals. There have been major efforts by lovers of liberty to counter these attacks. Perhaps the most successful has been "the underground economy," the subject of this book.

# Under the Table and Into Your Pocket
## The How and Why of the Underground Economy

4

# Why Paying Taxes is Un-American

Traditional American democracy recognizes the right of each person to act as he chooses, so long as he doesn't violate the rights of others. This is radically different from the philosophies that undergird other countries' approaches to government and commerce.

## The Right to Defy an Unjust Government

French King Louis XIV was fond of saying about himself "L'etat, c'est moi," which translates to "I am the state." In stating this he was invoking absolutism: the belief that government's power over the people is unlimited and cannot be challenged. This attitude is still held in many parts of the world.

Many Americans have adopted this same attitude. Fortunately there are still freedom-loving citizens who cling to self-reliance and distrust government. In spite of Washington's best efforts, people living in the U.S. still enjoy a level of personal and economic freedom unknown anywhere else in the world.

This is because the Founding Fathers rejected the idea that governments possess any sort of "divine right" to control the masses. Instead they envisioned the governing relationship between the people and their "rulers" as a "social contract," an idea proposed by philosophers such as Jean-Jacques Rousseau and Thomas Hobbes in the 17th and 18th centuries. It is summed up in these words from the Declaration of Independence:

> We hold these truths to be self-evident, that all men are created equal, that they are endowed by their Creator with certain unalienable Rights, that among these are Life, Liberty

## Chapter One
## Foundations of A Free Economy

and the pursuit of Happiness. That to secure these rights, Governments are instituted among Men, deriving their just powers from the consent of the governed, that whenever any Form of Government becomes destructive of these ends, it is the Right of the People to alter or to abolish it, and to institute new Government, laying its foundation on such principles and organizing its powers in such form, as to them shall seem most likely to effect their Safety and Happiness.

It is difficult for us in the 21$^{st}$ century to realize just how radical these words were at the time they were written. For the first time since the ancient Greek and Roman republics', government was seen as the *servant* of the people; not the other way around. Furthermore, the State's power was contingent on it fulfilling its end of the bargain with the people. If it failed in this regard, the people were free to alter it or, if necessary, to abolish it through revolution.

### The Individual vs. the State

New wealth is created continuously by inventors, business people and entrepreneurs. As long as human beings are free to create, invent and develop, the economic "pie" will continue to grow, allowing everyone a chance at a bigger slice. The real danger isn't private enterprise, it is government controls and taxation.

Free enterprise is like the kudzu weeds that infest so much of the southeast; it pops up, seemingly out of nowhere, in the most barren of places, and spreads like wildfire as long as no one poisons it.

On Saturday mornings I can drive past virtually any large field or parking lot in my area, and see entrepreneurs offering goods for sale out of the beds of pickup trucks or the trunks of their cars. The items being sold range from furniture, jewelry, artwork and clothing to books, garden produce, novelty items

# Under the Table and Into Your Pocket
## The How and Why of the Underground Economy

6

and locally made crafts. Often they set up shop right in front of a business that has closed down, bringing new economic life to the abandoned property.

Sometimes their wares are the products of their own hands, other times they were purchased for resale or are simply things the owner no longer wants. While there is tremendous variety in the goods being sold, there are strong commonalities among those doing the selling. They are all free human beings, freely engaging in trade with other human beings, to the mutual profit of all.

I recently bought a used vacuum cleaner from such a dealer. The cost was thirty dollars. The trade was advantageous to us both, because one needed the cash more than the product, the other vice versa. It was a "win-win" situation for both parties. It is the nature of capitalism to provide all parties with the things they desire.

Inherent in free trade is the principle that value of goods or a service is subjective; that is, worth whatever someone is willing to pay for it. For example, one person may look at a Mickey Mantle baseball card from the 1950's and see nothing more than a faded photograph on a piece of cardboard, not worth two cents. Another may think it more valuable than all the tea in China. One consumer may spend a large portion of his income on a luxury automobile, another on stock options. The point is that each obtains what brings them pleasure and satisfaction; thus, each is a winner.

It is such blatantly capitalistic practices that have made the United States the most productive nation on earth. The U.S. has a gross domestic product twice that of its nearest competitor. Compared to their European and Japanese counterparts, American workers take home more pay after taxes, enjoy access to a cheaper and wider variety of consumer goods, and

## Chapter One
## Foundations of A Free Economy

outstrip them in such measures of wealth as home ownership[1]. American free enterprise has accomplished far more good for its citizens than the planned economies of the Old World, while allowing them unparalleled freedom in all areas of life.

### The Good News

Even in these times of onerous government taxation and regulation there remains a core group of Americans who remain true to the principles upon which this Republic was founded. They consider themselves free individuals. They engage in voluntary commerce, offering products and services that are beneficial to others. They may be electricians, ditch diggers, physicians, merchants, janitors, engineers, or members of a host of other legal and honorable professions. But they are united by a fierce desire to protect their basic economic liberties from the encroachment of the government.

These people are true patriots. They honor the spirit and ideals of the Founding Fathers. They celebrate and exercise their natural rights, without assaulting those of others. They are not the shady, selfish miscreants that you read about in articles criticizing the underground economy. They are your friends and neighbors, making their homes, communities and nation better places. They are the economic heroes of the 21st century. It is to them this book is dedicated.

Many people see government control as a necessary counter balance against the growing power of corporations. They have legitimate concerns about business practices that exploit workers and damage the environment. I share those concerns. However, I also maintain that the people have the power to counter these forces on their own, through the use of two powerful tools: the strike and the boycott. Informed and active citizens are far more capable of protecting their interests than any government agency.

## Chapter Two
## Taxes, Licenses, Monopolies, Oh My!

*"Many of you benefited from the recent tax cuts, and we're going to cut that short. We're going to take things away from you on behalf of the common good."* — Senator Hillary Clinton, speaking to a group of wealthy taxpayers in San Francisco, June 8, 2004

*"The next time you encounter one of those "public-spirited" dreamers who tells you that that 'some very desirable goals cannot be achieved without everybody's participation,' tell him that if he cannot obtain everybody's voluntary participation, his goals had jolly well remain unachieved — and that men's lives are not his to dispose of."* — Ayn Rand, *The Virtue of Selfishness*

### Working for The Man

Imagine this: it's payday for you and you're walking out of the bank. You've just cashed your check, and you're looking forward to spending the money you toiled for all week.

As you head to your car, you're stopped by a group of men in dark suits pointing guns at you. "Gimme your wallet!" one growls. Trembling, you hand it over. He passes it to a fellow standing behind him, a white male in his forties, average height, with a little bit of a paunch and graying hair. He's wearing an expensive suit, and a limousine is parked on the

# Under the Table and Into Your Pocket
## The How and Why of the Underground Economy

street beside him. He pulls out several large bills and puts them in his pocket.

Your temper flares, and you're tempted to fight, but you're outnumbered and unarmed. After several minutes the man hands the wallet back to the thug that took it, who returns it to you. Confused and terrified, you count the bills that remain. You left the bank with five hundred dollars, but now there's only three hundred and fifty left.

"You dirty bastard!" you scream at their gang leader. "I need that money! I worked my ass off for it! Give it back to me!" He regards you with a smug, condescending smile, and then says, "Well, I could do that, of course. But you might not spend it right!" His remark leaves you stunned and speechless, and you watch as he and his entourage get in the limo and ride off.

You might laugh at the above story, thinking it could never occur. But the sad truth is that it *has* happened to you, time after time, since you first started working for a living. Americans pay an average of thirty percent of their income to local, state and federal government. In fact, when various excise and other taxes are figured in, many citizens are having over *forty percent* of their money stolen by government.[1]

And every penny of this largesse was taken without your consent. You don't notice it because the government is crafty in how it robs you. It uses tricks like income tax withholding, as well as indirect taxes, which are levied on manufacturers and service providers, who in turn pass the cost on to you.

When you realize just how much of your earnings are being taken, the preceding story doesn't seem all that farfetched. By the way, the creeps in dark suits with guns represent the IRS, which has the power to forcibly take your money, your pos-

---

[1] Gross, Martin L. *The Federal Tax Racket*, p.2.

Chapter Two
*Taxes, Licenses, Monopolies, Oh My!*

sessions, and your freedom if you don't cough up what they demand.

## The Sad History of Taxation in America

In the early years of the United States there were few taxes. What money the government needed to fulfill its limited constitutional objectives was provided through charges on carriages, tobacco, sugar and other items. The people were quick to act against federal attempts to place unfair levies on them (for example, the Whiskey Tax Rebellion in the summer of 1794, led by western Pennsylvania residents upset with taxes on homemade liquor).[2]

The country was largely made up of Scotch-Irish immigrants, who had a long tradition of valuing independence and distrusting government. They had a healthy confidence in their abilities to take care of their own, and sought neither "help" nor interference from Washington. It is from such fine stock the author of this book descended.

The War of 1812 created additional costs for the military, which resulted in new taxes on gold, silverware, jewelry and watches. These were repealed by Congress in 1817. (Imagine, Congress *eliminating* taxes!) Soon after, all internal taxes were abolished, and tariffs on imported goods became Washington's only source of revenue.

In 1862 the military again faced a budget crunch, due to the War Between the States. In that year Congress established the first income tax. It set taxes on people earning from six hundred to ten thousand dollars a year at the obscene rate of three percent. A Commissioner of Internal Revenue was established, who had the power to assess and collect taxes, and to punish

---

[2] http://www.britannica.com/eb/article?tocId=9076786

## Under the Table and Into Your Pocket
### The How and Why of the Underground Economy

non-compliers. This lasted until 1872, when Uncle Sam again abolished the income tax.

Over the next forty one years numerous attempts to establish a permanent income tax were made, but its advocates faced a formidable opponent: the Constitution, which would not allow it. Finally, in 1913 the sixteenth amendment made the tax a permanent part of life in the USA. Federal coffers swelled, as rates rose as high as seventy seven percent, before coming down in the 1920's. They went up again during the Great Depression.[3]

The income tax was sold as a way to "soak the rich." For its first thirty years or so it was applied only to those in high income brackets, and was paid in an annual lump sum.

President Kennedy reduced rates during his administration. Since the 1960's they have gone up and down in a seesaw pattern, but, on average, families currently pay twice the percentage of their income in taxes as what they paid in the past.

### A Law Against This, A Law Against That

All Sabrina Reece wanted was to make a living doing something she enjoyed. A resident of Compton, California, she was the owner of Braids by Sabrina, a small shop where she practiced the ancient African art of hair braiding. Her trade involves arranging hair in highly decorative fashions using only the designer's hands and some simple tools. There is no cutting of the hair and no chemicals are involved.

Her service was popular with local ladies. Sabrina herself was a productive and law abiding member of the community. This didn't protect her from the long arm of Big Brother, however.

---

[3] http://www.britannica.com/eb/article?tocId=9108612>

## Chapter Two
### Taxes, Licenses, Monopolies, Oh My!

On July 1, 1998, a woman and her "husband" came into the shop. The wife paid Sabrina $150.00 to braid her hair. After the job was done she asked to use her restroom. Her customer came out seconds later, wearing a badge and carrying a gun. Then a cop burst into the salon from the street, screaming at Sabrina and waving a piece of paper in her face. "He told me I'd go to jail if I didn't sign it," she related later. Her great crime? California requires hair braiders to hold cosmetology licenses, and Sabrina didn't have one. For this she was the target of a "hair sting." Later she was fined $1,000.00.

In California a cosmetology license costs $6,000.00 to $9,000.00 to obtain, along with 1600 hours of schooling. For many poor and minority entrepreneurs this presents an impossible hurdle. Furthermore there is not one shred of information on hair braiding in the standard cosmetology curriculum.[4]

Women like Sabrina are forced to spend thousands of dollars and get hundreds of hours of training in a subject that has nothing to do with their occupation. This is one example of how government regulations are crippling businesses and robbing people of the chance to become self-sufficient. Unfortunately it's only one of thousands.

### Government Poisons the Drinking Water

The regulatory situation in California is so bad that it takes years longer for businesses to do the simplest things. For example, in most states it takes four to six months to open a new gas station, from the day the permit is applied for to the grand opening. In the Golden State in takes an average of three years.

The bureaucrats in the state capitol pride themselves on their commitment to the environment. Unfortunately their zeal isn't

---

[4] www.salon.com/news/feature/1999/09/13/hair/

always based on fact. In the 1990s petroleum producers in the state were required to start adding a chemical called MTBE to gas. At first the substance was hailed as a miracle; it boosted octane and reduced toxic emissions.

Further study found it to be highly carcinogenic, though. What's worse, large quantities of it have leeched into the water supply from leaking tanks. So when you go to California bring your own $H_2O$. The politicians have poisoned the local stuff.[5]

## Atlas Shrugs in the Golden State

Because of nonsense like the above, 40% of the businesses in California plan to pull out of the state, according to a recent study by the Bain Institute. And most of those jobs aren't going overseas. Sixty percent are going to business-friendly areas in the U.S.

Texas is a big winner in this exodus. Thousands of new jobs are being created there by companies fleeing the flood of new regulations flowing out of Sacramento. If John Galt were alive today he might choose the Lone Star State for his refuge, rather than the mountains of Colorado.[6]

Of course, California isn't the only place where those who create jobs and wealth are being punished. Let's travel across the country to that Mecca of socialist thought, New York City.

## Killing Entrepreneurship in the Big Apple

Jorge Hernandez was a recent immigrant to America who wanted to own a taxi service in New York City. He was a pro-

---

[5] www.dhs.ca.gov/ps/ddwem/chemicals/MTBE/**mtbe**index.htm
[6] republican.sen.ca.gov/news/99/pressrelease2367.asp

## Chapter Two
### *Taxes, Licenses, Monopolies, Oh My!*

fessional driver back in Mexico and enjoyed the work. So he set out to city hall to find out how to get started.

The clerk informed him that he would have to obtain a "medallion," the term for a cab permit. "Okay," he said, reaching for his wallet, "how much are they?" The sour faced woman behind the desk looked up at him and said, "Well, you have to buy them at auction. On average they go for $227,000." Jorge dropped his wallet and grabbed his chest.

Being a determined sort, he kept pursuing his dream. He found a company that would finance the medallion purchase for him, went to auction and got one. Now he became excited, thinking of all those big fares he would pick up in Manhattan. Good times were just around the corner, he figured.

That was five years ago. He is five years into the 15-year repayment period for his medallion. He works fourteen hours a day, seven days a week to cover his expenses. This leaves him an average wage of six bucks an hour to live on, a pitiful amount indeed to survive on in the most expensive city on earth.

At least Jorge has his health. And he'd better keep it. If he gets sick and can't work for a month or two he will go into default on his medallion payments. The bank will take it away and sell it to another bidder. Jorge will have nothing to show for all the years he put in, since he acquires no equity as he pays the loan off.

Jorge's story is typical of what aspiring cabbies have to deal with in New York City. They're not alone. Street merchants and other entrepreneurs routinely have their dreams crushed by a system mired in red tape that punishes ambition.

The historic image of New York is one of hard working immigrants moving to the city from all over the world, and pulling themselves up to prosperity by their own bootstraps. However, that ain't the way it is these days. In a city where ten percent of the residents are on welfare, the powers that be

## Under the Table and Into Your Pocket
### The How and Why of the Underground Economy

seem determined to cut those boot straps off and keep people from rising above poverty.

There are three main ways that aspiring small business owners are crippled by regulations in the Big Apple:
- Ceilings on the number of business permits issued. These affect taxis, street vendors and newsstand owners.
- Occupational licenses — with requirements far out of proportion to the level of skills needed to perform the occupation, for example, restrictions on hair braiders similar to those in California.
- Public monopolies — just try starting a private trash pick up service inside the city, for example.

By law no more than 4,000 food vendors and 1,700 merchandise vendors can operate on the streets. Food vendors are forced to take the city's course on food prep no matter their level of education or experience in sanitation or restaurant work. They then must buy a decal for their cart. The number of decals sold is strictly limited by the city.

This has led to domination of the trade by a group of corporations that buys decaled carts and leases them to individuals. The price structure is set up to keep the vendors poor and the corporate executives rich. Both food and merchandise vendors must buy an extra permit if they want to sell in the city's parks. Prices for this permit range from $500 to $228,000 a year.

In 1993 a group of African-American women in Brooklyn formed a self-help group to improve their economic lot. As one of their efforts, they started a catering business. Lacking a commercial kitchen they prepared the food in their homes. The city brought its wrath down on them for daring to do so.

It wasn't the cleanliness or condition of the kitchens the city was pissed about. They could have been as sterile as an operating room. They were still condemned simply because they were in private homes. This is despite the fact that caterers are

## Chapter Two
### Taxes, Licenses, Monopolies, Oh My!

allowed to use their home kitchens in most states in the U.S., provided they pass a basic sanitation inspection.

Another classic business for cash-starved entrepreneurs, home childcare, is desperately needed in New York City with its large number of single working parents. Unfortunately this is yet another enterprise that the city smothers with absurd regulations.

For example, the manager of a childcare service is required to hold a master's degree. This means that my own good mother, who brought up eight healthy children on a shoestring budget, couldn't keep kids in her home.

A horde of other ridiculous rules choke off other enterprises, keeping the poor dependent on government assistance. Those who do break free of the welfare system most often resort to that most wonderful of American establishments, the underground economy. For example, there are an estimated 30,000 "gypsy" cabbies in the city that operate without medallions.

In addition there are limousine and car services that do double duty as taxis, picking up people that hail them from the street, though doing so is against city law. I have a friend who travels to the City frequently on business. He almost always uses one of the "illegal" services over the medallion cabs. He reports that the drivers are courteous and knowledgeable and the fares a bargain.

Most people would agree it makes sense for, say, an airline pilot or a brain surgeon to be licensed in their professions. But what about the guy who sells tickets at the theater? In New York they must be licensed by the city. One must also obtain a license to shovel snow, open a thrift store, or charge people to park in a vacant lot.

Want to start a private garbage pickup service in Manhattan or one of the other boroughs? Forget it. There are a plethora of

# Under the Table and Into Your Pocket
## The How and Why of the Underground Economy

services that the city controls through legal monopoly, including sanitation.[7]

## Regulations are Killing Businesses Nationwide

Don't try to fill your car's tank in New Jersey. It could get you arrested. Service stations in the Garden State are required to pump gas for their customers, driving up costs by forcing them to hire additional personnel. Ditto for Oregon.

Want to open a tattoo shop? Forget about South Carolina. The state has a ban on body art clearly derived from religious bias. For example, a state senator who defended the statute said "If God wanted you to have a tattoo, you would have been born with one.... here in South Carolina, we still believe in God." He went on to say that he might change his mind if the leader of the state Baptist convention said tattoos were okay.[8]

There is hope, though. Defying the edicts of parasitic bureaucrats and idiot politicians is a group of Americans, millions of them, who have thrown off the yoke of state slavery and embraced economic freedom. They operate right under the nose of the enemy, buying and selling, offering and taking services, and building their personal wealth while benefiting others through free and mutual trade. As our society crumbles under the weight of the looters these brave souls keep alive the promise of liberty that is every citizen's birthright.

We'll take a closer look at them in this book. We'll study how they subvert the silly rules that would drive them into poverty. We'll meet a few face to face. And we'll learn that not only do Americans hate paying taxes to a cruel, backwards and sadistic government, but they've also found ingenious

---

[7] www.ij.org
[8] www.cfarfreedom.org/tattoo.shtml

## Chapter Two
### Taxes, Licenses, Monopolies, Oh My!

ways to fight for freedom right under the nose of the collectivist tyrants.

In the last chapter we looked at why Americans resist paying taxes. We saw how the very idea of the income tax is contrary to the principles upon which the United States is founded. We examined how government has declared war on the entrepreneurial spirit by over-regulating business.

Next we'll see how citizens are fighting back. We'll learn about the IRS by taking a brief look at its history, structure and methods. We'll also expose its weaknesses, and how economic patriots exploit them to enhance their freedom.

We'll look at the pros and cons of working tax-free. We'll discuss things one must do to succeed in the underground economy and some things the aspiring tax resistor must *never* do. Finally we'll study issues anyone should consider when working outside the "safety zone" of conventional employment, such as obtaining health insurance and planning for retirement.

## Chapter Three
## Feeding the Tax Monster

*"We must not let our rulers load us with perpetual debt. We must make our election between economy and liberty or profusion and servitude. If we run into such debt, as that we must be taxed in our meat and in our drink, in our necessaries and our comforts, in our labors and our amusements, for our calling and our creeds... we [will] have no time to think, no means of calling our miss-managers to account but be glad to obtain subsistence by hiring ourselves to rivet their chains on the necks of our fellow-sufferers. And this is the tendency of all human governments. A departure from principle in one instance becomes a precedent... till the bulk of society is reduced to be mere automatons of misery. And the fore-horse of this frightful team is public debt. Taxation follows that, and in its train wretchedness and oppression."* — Thomas Jefferson

### Know Thy Enemy

*"The goal of American lawmakers has always been to balance the need to raise revenue, the desire to be fair to taxpayers, and the desire to influence the way taxpayers save and spend their money."* — quote from the IRS official web site, www.irs.gov

From the brief history of the IRS in the last chapter, we learned how it grew from a tiny, temporary operation to a monstrous beast. We saw how it feeds the government's lust for our money. Now we're going to look at its size, structure, and methods of operation.

## The Nature of the Beast

The Internal Revenue Service is enormous. It has almost 100,000 full time employees and a budget of over ten billion dollars. It commands an army of accountants, attorneys and investigators. Though their individual job descriptions may vary, each of them has a single overarching goal: to make sure you pay every penny they say you owe to Uncle Sam. They are cruel, efficient and relentless in pursuing this goal.

The IRS is split into four main divisions:
- The Wage and Investment Division — "serving" the 116 million taxpayers who file returns.
- The Small Business/Self-Employed Division — which deals with over 45 million small businesses and self-employed persons.
- The Large and Mid-Size Business Division — responsible for collecting tribute from corporations with assets exceeding $10 million.
- The Tax-Exempt and Government Entities Division — oversees employee benefit plans, tax-exempt organizations, and government entities.

Sub-divisions include Appeals, Communications and Criminal Investigation.

## The Bounty

The IRS is quite simply the best collection agency on planet Earth. The following stats show how much money it exacted from the people for fiscal year 2003. Figures are from the IRS web site (www.irs.gov) and are in millions of dollars.

## Chapter Three
### Feeding the Tax Monster

Individual Income Taxes ................................................ $987,209
Corporate Income Taxes ............................................... $194,146
Employment Taxes ....................................................... $695,976
Gift Taxes .......................................................................... $1,939
Excise Taxes ..................................................................... $52,771
Estate Taxes ................................................................. $20,888[1]

    The total haul: One trillion, nine hundred and fifty two billion, nine hundred and twenty nine million dollars! To give some perspective on much money that really is, imagine a stack of one dollar bills 125,000 miles high. It would reach halfway to the moon. It would wrap around the globe five times.

    If you were to spend this amount at the rate of one thousand dollars a second it would take you fifteen hundred years, a millennium and a half, to do so. That's how much money the government received last year.

    And it still can't balance its books.

    Looking at the above shows just how the tax code has wormed its way into every aspect of citizens' lives. Not only are employees taxed, but also companies of all sizes, recipients of gifts and inheritors of estates. On top of that there are excise levies on gasoline, alcohol, cigarettes, automobiles, firearms, telephone service, etc., etc. *ad nauseum.*[2] God help the poor fellow who smokes, drinks, drives a luxury car, owns guns, uses a phone, and runs his own business!

    There is virtually no economic activity from which the government parasites don't leech. They are like the "looters" Ayn Rand described in *Atlas Shrugged.* Unable or unwilling to cre-

---

[1] www.irs.gov
[2] Gross, Martin *The Tax Racket* p. 116

ate wealth themselves, they steal it from those who do, giving sickness, decay and death in exchange.

## A History of Abuse, Arrogance, and Asshole Behavior

The IRS has long been known for its arrogant, condescending attitude, its flagrant abuse of taxpayers, and its refusal to accept accountability for its actions. In 1998 Congress held a series of hearings, inviting both taxpayers as well as IRS employees to share their horror stories about the agency. Many of the accounts that surfaced were chilling:

- While enduring an audit, Carole Ward had enough of the IRS representative's stupidity. She told the moron "Honey, from what I can see of your accounting skills, the country would be better served if you were dishing up chicken-fried steak on some interstate in West Texas." Way to exercise those First Amendment rights, Carole!

  Response from the IRS was both immediate and brutal. A few days after the audit they raided her son's business, padlocked the doors and demanded $325,000 in alleged "back taxes" from Ward. They also leaked confidential information about her to the press.

  This was the beginning of a legal and financial nightmare for Ward. It would stretch over several years, cost her hundreds of thousands of dollars and cause her endless aggravation and worry.

  Carole Ward refused to crumble under the pressure, however. In June of 1997, she won a $325,000 judgment against the agency, the same amount they falsely accused her of owing them. The presiding justice in the case, U.S. District Judge William Downes, said after the trial "By this award, this court gives notice to the IRS that reprehensible abuse by one of its employees cannot and will not be tolerated."

## Chapter Three
### Feeding the Tax Monster

Despite her victory, Ward was exhausted and emotionally devastated by the ordeal. "It would be wonderful if I felt like dancing on graves," she said. "But by the time you get the victory it doesn't feel like one. They take out the joy."[3]

- Stanley McGill was suffering from dementia when, at the age of 93, he overpaid his taxes by a full $7,000. The IRS cheerfully took the man's money. A few years later his granddaughter discovered the mistake, and kindly asked for the money back. The IRS acknowledged that the money wasn't rightfully theirs. They then refused to give it back, stating that refund requests must be made within three years.

  The granddaughter challenged the IRS ruling, taking the case all the way to the US Supreme Court. She lost. The justices unanimously ruled that the government could keep the money. Writing for the court, Justice Stephen G. Breyer said that such occasional unfair actions were necessary "to maintain a more workable tax enforcement system." One wonders how the Court would have ruled if the tables were turned and Mr. McGill owed $7,000 to the IRS.[4]

- An unnamed IRS employee brought a case against U.S. Senator Howard Baker, accusing him of tax evasion and presenting "proof" of the charge. The frame-up unraveled when IRS agent Tommy Henderson found that the evidence was obviously fabricated. It was later revealed that the IRS employee who leveled the charges was trying to score brownie points with the agency by scoring a "bust" against a prominent person.[5]

- Representative David Skaggs, D-Colorado, was upset when some of his Republican colleagues criticized a liberal think tank he was fond of. So he asked the IRS to retaliate by har-

---

[3] www.lubbockonline.com/news/060697/judge.htm
[4] www.worldnetdaily.com/news/article.asp?ARTICLE_ID=14327
[5] www.cnn.com/ALLPOLITICS/1998/04/30/**irs**.hearings/

assing the conservative group the Heritage Foundation. The agency complied, launching a series of investigations into the foundation that ultimately cost it over $100,000 in legal fees. A resulting lawsuit brought by the Landmark Legal Foundation found that the IRS had initiated the audits purely as a personal favor to Skaggs.[6]
- Ernest Kugler, Jr. spent a decade fighting the IRS over taxes the agency said he owed from his heating and cooling business. Kugler filed for bankruptcy four times but his tax liability kept growing, swelling to over $115,000. The IRS refused to work with Kugler on a payment plan.

On May 15, he told his wife that he could not face another meeting with the tax collectors. His body was discovered four days later in his pickup truck in a wooded area. He had committed suicide via carbon monoxide poisoning, driven to unbearable despair by the IRS.[7]

Many of the people who testified during the hearings were IRS employees who were tired of the corruption they saw in the agency. They testified behind screens and spoke into devices that altered their voices. They were terrified that the agency would come after them for spilling the beans.

According to the House Ways and Means Committee, the IRS tax code is 1.3 million words long and covers well over nine thousand pages. The result is that even veteran tax attorneys do not understand it, leaving collectors free to interpret it as they choose. Because of this almost god-like power they can target virtually any U.S. citizen for harassment, citing their "failure" to comply with some obscure sub-section buried in the text.

As a result of the hearings, Congress passed the IRS Restructuring and Reform Act of 1998. The law expands tax-

---

[6] www.landmarklegal.org/latest_ developments.cfm?webpage_id=488
[7] www.thevanguard.org/thevanguard/ issues/flat_tax/horror_stories.shtml

## Chapter Three
## Feeding the Tax Monster

payer rights and ostensibly curbs the agency's powers. However, reports indicate that the IRS continues with its old ways, still abusing taxpayers and flaunting the law.[8]

This isn't surprising. The agency serves a corrupt, immoral federal government with a history of molesting its subjects. Only by abolishing the IRS will Americans be free of its tyranny.

The good news is that the underground economy continues to thrive. For example, in 1995 it was estimated that $630 billion dollars in income went unreported and untaxed. IRS Commissioner Charles Rosotti says that the federal government is losing almost $200 billion a year in tax revenue due to economic patriotism.[9]

That's a lot of money that's being kept in the private sector, where it can do some good. Uncle Sam would just waste it on pork barrel projects, handouts to deadbeats, grants to fascist police departments or weapons systems for our imperialistic military. Let's hear it for the guerilla capitalists!

In fact, chances are that you, dear reader, have participated in the underground economy. Ever sold something without reporting the income? Performed a service such as electrical work or plumbing without the mandatory licenses? Paid someone cash to cut your grass, prune your hedges or wash your car? Bought something from a street peddler? Chances are that every adult in this country has dipped their fingers into this tax-free bonanza at one point or another.

---

[8] www.tax-freedom.com/termination.htm
[9] www.ncpa.org/ba/ba273.html

# Under the Table and Into Your Pocket
## The How and Why of the Underground Economy

## Is It For Me?

At this point you may be ready to jump into the underground economy lock, stock and barrel. However there are many things to consider first.

We all agree that taxes are an abomination. Having established that, realize that there are two ways to get out of paying them: one is outright evasion, where you just refuse to play by the rules at all. The other is avoidance, where you aggressively take advantage of every legal means possible to reduce or eliminate your tax burden.

From a financial perspective working underground may or may not be for you. The simple truth is that for many individuals, it makes more sense to work within the system, unless you have a very strong moral objection to paying income tax. Whether or not this is true for you depends on many factors:

- What is the nature of the work you want to do? Some vocations lend themselves much more easily to the underground economy than others. For example, one or two person gigs like house cleaning, trash hauling, desktop publishing, etc. are fairly safe.

  On the other hand, jobs where you will need helpers can be problematic. Each person who works with you is a potential liability, especially if they are injured on the job or decide to turn you in to the IRS. Since you will not be able to provide such standard benefits as workman's compensation insurance, the fewer workers the better.

- Additionally, you need to consider the amount of liability your work exposes you to. Selling jewelry and watches on a street corner is a low risk profession. The worst thing you are likely to encounter is a PO'ed customer who wants their money back. On the other hand, an architect's potential liability is huge, if his designs are later determined to be de-

## Chapter Three
### Feeding the Tax Monster

fective. Doing such work underground only exacerbates that.
- What hurdles do you need to leap through to go into business legally? Again, this can depend on many factors that vary from state to state. For example, in some there are very few requirements to become a private investigator. Others require extensive backgrounds checks as well as many hours of prior work in law enforcement or security.

  This factor is influenced not only by state and federal laws but also by such mundane things as homeowner covenants. For example, many subdivisions forbid various types of home-based businesses. Evaluate all the rules you will have to obey before you decide to go underground.
- What tax deductions can you take by staying aboveground? This is a vital point to consider, since the simple truth is that many who choose to work underground could actually come out further ahead by playing by the rules. There is a plethora of ways for business people to cut their tax burden. Read a good book or two on the deductions available, or better yet invest some time and money in talking to a good attorney or accountant.
- If you are considering working underground full time, you will have to decide what to do about insurance, retirement funds, and other benefits that "legitimate" employees and business owners enjoy. Can you provide for your own health and life insurance? Are you comfortable saving for tomorrow by squirreling away cash? Do you want to have a foreign bank account and/or investments? We'll discuss insurance and investments in detail a little later on.
- How comfortable are you with skirting the law? Some people go their entire lives flouting the legal system and never lose a moment's sleep. Others still worry that the cops are going to bust them for that doobie they took a toke on in

1965. Figure out which kind of person you are before going underground.

Okay, you've searched your soul, looked at all the factors, and decided that you want to work in the underground economy. Let's look at getting your feet wet.

# Chapter Four
# The Buck Starts Here

### Breaking In

Certain basic principles govern all economic activity, underground or not. First off, you must recognize that total self-sufficiency is an illusion. Some romantics have fantasized about buying a piece of land deep in the woods and cutting off all ties to civilization. "We'll grow our own food," they say, "and build our home from the trees we cut down. We'll weave our own cloth, sew our own clothes, and even make our own soap from animal fats and ashes. We'll burn torches or make tallow candles for light, and wear animal skins for warmth. We'll need no one."

Get real. Even the pioneers and American Indians didn't live that way. They actively engaged in barter. For example, the Cherokee used to walk from their home in the southern Appalachians to what is now Ohio. They exchanged rare gems and stones for a mineral called mica, which was naturally transparent. It could be cut into flat sheets and used to make windows for their huts. The Scotch-Irish hill people of the same area brewed moonshine in large quantities, not just to drink themselves, but to trade for finished goods brought in by mule trains.

In order to survive you must *trade*. Employees trade time, effort and skill for paychecks. Manufacturers trade finished goods for money. Gold diggers trade marital bliss for security. Even panhandlers and clergymen take money in exchange for warm fuzzy feelings. Only criminals and politicians can prosper by taking and not giving back.

Also, you need to realize that no matter what you do for a living you are in business. Employees often fool themselves into thinking otherwise because of the controls they allow their bosses to place on them. In reality, though, they are doing the same thing the business owner is doing: offering a product or service for sale on the open market.

And they have no more security than he or she does. If their customer (the company they work for) decides that they no longer want or need their product or service, then they're out the door, simple as that.

## There is no security, only opportunities.

So to make a living off the books you must first have a good or service that is in demand. You must then find a way to sell it for money or exchange it for other goods or services. You must do so in a way that is untraceable and you must keep a low profile, lest you draw the attention of the taxman.

There are three levels of participation in the underground economy:

1. The casual user — those who make the vast majority of their income through legal means, but dabble in yard sales, babysitting, etc., on an occasional basis.
2. The sideliner — those who work a regular job or own an aboveground business, but who often supplement their reported income with cash-only transactions. Lawyers, doctors, mechanics, caterers, carpenters, plumbers, electricians, even merchants often take this route. A variation on this is the waiter or waitress who doesn't report his tips.
3. The full time mole — works totally off the books. You might think this is the domain of the Mafia and other professional criminals. However, some legitimate professions are fairly easy to work on a cash basis, example: personal

## Chapter Four
## The Buck Starts Here

care provider/companion, general handyman, dominatrix, professional beggar, street musician, peddler, fortune teller/spiritual advisor, exotic dancer.

Let's look at the pros and cons of these options. The first one entails the least risk by far. As mentioned before, virtually everyone has flirted with the underground economy at one time or another. The person who does occasional side work or runs a low-key business like a flea market stand will probably enjoy years of untraceable extra income without the slightest fear of a knock at the door from the IRS. The politician who pays his nanny or housekeeper under the table saves the bookwork and payroll taxes.

As little as a couple hundred extra dollars a month can enhance one's life significantly. For people on the edge of poverty it can be a way to pay the light bill and feed the kids. For the more affluent it can mean nicer clothes, a weekend getaway or a few good restaurant meals. This much cash can be brought in by cutting a few lawns, selling junk sitting in your garage, or baking cakes and pies for others.

More money can be made by the person who invests a significant amount of time working on the side, either selling products or doing service work. For skilled blue-collar workers this is a bonanza. Virtually everyone needs electrical, plumbing, carpentry or auto repair work done. For those who lack a trade, local community colleges as well as correspondence courses offer training in fields like floral arrangement, bookkeeping and lawnmower/small engine repair. Knowledge of any of these can lead to big bucks in nearly any community in the U.S.

There is somewhat more risk with this option that the first, but there is little to fear as long as you do what this chapter recommends. Working regularly on a cash basis can lead to plenty of savings or to a more comfortable lifestyle for someone who already has a full time job. It can also provide a full-time income for those who can only find part-time work in the "legal" economy.

Working completely underground entails far more caution than the first two options. To stay out of trouble it is important that one live modestly. Things someone else could get away with, such as buying a home or new car, could get the undergrounder in hot water fast. This, along with the fact that a completely tax-free income can limit what you do for a living (since licenses and employees are out of the question) makes this option the least desirable for most people.

On the other hand, there are many who may find it quite attractive. For example, there are millions of people who dream of living in the rural Northwest, along the beaches of New England or in the Appalachian mountain region. But when they investigate moving they are discouraged by the lack of economic opportunities in such areas.

An underground enterprise may provide them with a decent income in the place of their choice, as long as they live modestly. I live in the rural south, and know firsthand that many, many people survive this way. The majority are honest, good, hard-working folk who live simple but happy lives. Their self-sufficiency is a testament to the spirit of the early pioneers.

Others who may prefer this option are those who believe that paying income tax is inherently immoral, because of moral or religious convictions. Another group is retirees living on Social Security, who risk being penalized for earning even modest amounts of money. It is insane that seniors should be punished in this regard, but nonetheless they are.

Whatever the level of one's participation in the underground economy, there are certain basic rules one must follow to be successful:
1. Work only for cash, personal check or bartered goods.
2. Avoid a paper trail.
3. Maintain a low profile and keep your mouth shut.

## Chapter Four
## The Buck Starts Here

**Cash** is the preferred means of payment. It is anonymous and universally accepted. The American greenback is still the most stable and sought after currency in the world. It can be used to pay bills in person or exchanged for a money order. Buying from catalogs or online merchants can be accomplished by mailing in a money order.

The only drawback to cash is that if it is stolen or lost you're screwed. Keep it carefully stashed away and don't carry large sums on your person. Occasionally a fancy hotel will refuse cash, insisting for payment by credit or debit card. Tell them to go to hell and head for the nearest Motel 6. You get the same night's sleep for a lot less money.

Checks will work if they are cashed at the payer's bank. They should never be deposited into one's own account. Have them made out to you, not to a business entity. Observe the same rules when paying others by check.

Barter has been around for eons, and preceded currency as the primary means of exchange. It can still work today. For example, Joe Blow may be willing to paint his neighbor's house in exchange for his old Volkswagen Beetle. Suzie Q might babysit for her sister one night. Her sibling returns the favor by making her some fudge. Bob Jones might have a bust of Marilyn Monroe gathering dust in his attic. His buddy Tom Wainwright, a huge fan of the deceased actress, offers him a fishing pole for it. These transactions are untraceable and untaxable.

Inflation and taxation have given rise to barter clubs. Members post goods or services they have for exchange in an association newsletter or website. Interested parties contact them, offering their own products in trade. Membership fees, rules and other factors vary. You can find these groups on the Net by doing a search with the words "barter club."

The problem with barter is that there are no set values. You might think that your lawnmower is worth as much as that fishing boat you want, but the boat's owner may not agree. In most instances good old cash transactions beat trading actual goods. Everyone can agree that money has value, and items can be appraised against it reliably, example, the Blue Book used car prices that are used by banks and dealers.

**Creating a paper trail** will do you in quickly in the underground economy. By this I mean generating receipts, bills, records, etc., that record your business activities.

Not only should your income be in cash, but any purchases you make for your business must be made in cash and be untraceable.

For this reason you should avoid using a tax ID number, or for that matter a Sam's Club or similar membership card, when buying work-related things. Doing either of these will tie you to what you buy, creating a paper trail right to you. Any records you keep should be written, not kept in a computer or on a disk, and only you should know where those records are. If it's possible to do without them entirely you should.

What kind of business you are in will be a major factor in how deep you can delve into the underground economy. For example, there is just too much government paperwork tied in with titles, registration, insurance, financing, etc., to make a big tax-free income selling cars. At best you could get away with a handful of casual sales a year.

On the other hand there are plenty of tax-free opportunities in selling goods. A person who sews clothes, makes furniture, paints pictures, etc., has all the skills needed to make an underground income right now. Also there are companies that will sell you tools, jewelry, knives, video tapes, clothes, socks, shoes, clocks, etc., etc., in bulk at wholesale prices. You can pay in cash and pick up the goods at their warehouse, or mail a money order and have them shipped to you.

## Chapter Four
## The Buck Starts Here

There are many places where a part-time salesperson can set up shop without being hassled. Perhaps the best is your local swap meet or flea market. If you've never been to one of these you owe it to yourself to go. There is no better example of raw, unrestrained capitalism in the United States.

At the larger markets you can find dozens or even hundreds of people selling an incredible variety of goods. I buy produce, garden plants and flowers, books, tools and tee shirts on a regular basis at flea markets. The products are usually as good as what you would find at Wal-Mart, often better, and the prices can't be beat. Almost no one worries about collecting sales tax or reporting the profits from their trades.

Selling your own goods is easy. Tables can be had for anywhere from two to twenty dollars a day, depending on factors such as location, market size, and geography. There will be an office where you can reserve your table in advance.

Saturday and Sunday are the big selling days, so you'll want to get there early and have your stuff out, usually no later than 8 a.m. Bring cash to make change, bags for the items you sell, and a radio to listen to as well as a comfortable chair for yourself.

Flea markets and swap meets can be great ways to make good money. To learn more about them, I highly recommend the book, *How to Make Cash Money Selling at Swap Meets, Flea Markets, Etc.*, by Jordan L. Cooper, available from Loompanics. It's a treasure trove of information. Also see the appendix of this book, where I list companies that sell products wholesale.

Those who want to make money selling services face other challenges. In particular there is the issue of liability. For example, if you want to make money moving furniture you run the risk of dropping someone's 300-year-old curio cabinet or sending their antique oak desk flying down the stairs.

## Under the Table and Into Your Pocket
The How and Why of the Underground Economy

A good way to handle this is to tell potential customers up front that you self-insure your work up to a certain amount, say $3,500. Be sure and keep this amount in reserve in case you accidentally damage their property. Of course the degree to which this should concern you will depend on the service you provide. A person who prepares resumes has less to be concerned about than the underground electrician who wires a house for cash.

Let's talk about finding work. Even in the underground economy one can advertise within certain limits. For instance, it would be suicide to erect an interstate billboard that says *Big Joe's Budget Carpentry: I Screw the Tax Man and Pass the Savings On To You!* However, a poster put up on a phone pole or a public bulletin board carries little risk. Flyers can be printed up and handed out, and ads can be placed in local shopping papers for a minimal cost.

The best way to find customers is by word of mouth. Do good, honest work at a fair price for whoever will let you, and then ask them to recommend you to others. This is absolutely the best form of advertising available and it costs you nothing.

## Hired Help

If you are either just dabbling in the underground economy or supplementing income from your regular business, then there is little danger in hiring help, so long as they know nothing of your tax free enterprises. On the other hand, if your income is totally from underground sources, then I strongly advise against taking on other workers. Anyone who knows what you are up to is a potential snitch.

You may think that someone who is in as deep as you would not tell, but this isn't necessarily true. Law enforcement makes deals with small fry crooks all the time, giving them reduced

*Chapter Four*
*The Buck Starts Here*

sentences in exchange for testifying against the boss. Your current partner could end up being your accuser in court.

The whole issue of not telling anyone else what you're doing ties into the third basic principle we'll look at:

## Keeping a low profile

More so than anything else, violating this rule can lead you to disaster. When you are socking away tax-free bucks the temptation to spend big can be overwhelming. You may look around and see big screen TVs, fancy cars, nice homes, gold watches, etc. and say "Why not? I've earned it!"

And you have. But don't lose sight of the fact that, in the eyes of the law, you are a criminal. Plenty of people get away with working tax-free all the time, often with the full knowledge of the police.

The simple truth is that the cops are too busy chasing after real crooks to bother with a guy making cash on the side. That can change quickly if you start flaunting the fruits of your ill-gotten gain, though.

## What about Benefits?

This will only be an issue for those who wish to work totally underground. Most "legitimate" workers have access to perks above and beyond their paychecks. These can include bonuses, tuition reimbursement, jury duty pay, and paid vacations. But the most popular and important ones are health/life insurance and a 401K or other investment plan. You will either forego all of these or have to provide them yourself.

## Insurance

Health insurance is virtually a necessity in today's world. Employers know that their hirelings are unlikely to leave a job that provides it. That is why many of them offer coverage to their workers. They pick up all or most of the premium. They in turn get a price break from the insurance companies for signing up their employees en masse.

In recent years the cost of this benefit has skyrocketed. Many companies have cut back on the insurance they offer or eliminated it entirely. Costs have increased for people who buy their own coverage as well.

The reasons for this are complex and beyond the scope of this book. Suffice it to say that this can be a major challenge for all self-employed people, whether working tax free or not. It is something you must address.

If you have a spouse who can add you to their insurance for a reasonable cost, then do so. And count yourself lucky. This is almost always the best way to go when available.

However, not everyone has this option. The next thing to look at is buying your own coverage. Costs for health insurance vary enormously, depending on which state you live in, your overall health, if you are buying it just for yourself or for your family, etc.

In South Carolina a healthy adult can purchase a single policy for a little over a hundred dollars a month. This includes doctor visit co-pays, discount prescription drugs, and coverage for major things like broken bones and cancer. The same policy bought in New Jersey can run $350 a month or more.

People with diabetes or other conditions can find getting health insurance at all a challenge. At the very least they will pay significantly more than others. For example, I am a diabetic who buys his own coverage. I pay 30% more than a non-diabetic would for the same policy.

## Chapter Four
## The Buck Starts Here

You need to check with insurance providers in your area to find out what your situation is. You may be tempted to risk going without any coverage. I strongly advise against this. Even a bare bones major medical policy with a high deductible is far better than nothing.

If you are unable to obtain health insurance of any kind, there are still a few alternatives that can assist you. In recent years medical discount plans have popped up across the country. Unlike insurance, they will accept anyone.

Membership can range from ten dollars a month to almost a hundred, and both single and family plans are available. They can save you money on medical expenses. They often have hundreds of doctors in their networks as well as hospitals and pharmacies.

The catch is that you will pay more for doctor visits, medicines, etc., than with insurance. Typically plan members can save 10-30% of the regular price of treatment and drugs. If a doctor charges $120 full price for a visit, for example, you can save up to $36.

Though far from perfect, a discount plan can be better than nothing. It's important to look at them carefully, as scams have popped up. You can find out about them by doing a web search for "discount medical." Some of the better ones advertise on TV. Before buying check the company out with the Better Business Bureau.

Another good idea is to make sure they have a list of affiliated doctors on their web site. If they don't, then cross them off your list. If they do then call some of them to make sure they really are associated with the plan. Also make sure that they have doctors reasonably close to you.

There are other ways to reduce to cost of health care. For example, I live near one of the poorest counties in the Appalachians. When I was without insurance I called a medical clinic there, and found out that it only charged $50 per doctor visit versus the $100 plus in my town. I gladly drove the extra distance along twisting mountain roads to save the money.

Remember, medical care is like any other product or service. Its practitioners can only charge as much as the market will bear. Unfortunately, insurance co-pays have artificially inflated its costs, making things even harder on those without coverage.

## Investments

The dollar has one weakness: left to itself it loses value due to inflation. For example, when I was a very young child I could buy a comic book for twelve cents. Then the price hit fifteen cents, then twenty.

And on one dark day in the mid-1970s I went to the local drug store and saw that the new issue of *Weird Wonder Tales* was going to set me back a full quarter! Nowadays they run well over a buck — and the stories aren't as good.

You may stash away tens of thousands of dollars from your underground enterprises. But if you want those bucks to keep their value you must invest them. This can be challenging, since Uncle Sam requires you to report any money earned from stocks, bonds, savings accounts, etc.

Fear not, there is no reason for despair. There are ways to invest both discretely and profitably. We'll look at several of them in this section.

## Overseas Banking

Yes it is legal, and no, you don't have to be a drug kingpin to do it. You can open a checking and savings account in such stable countries as Canada, Austria and Sweden with a minimum of effort and expense. You will earn a decent rate of interest, enjoy protection of your funds, and even get a debit or

## Chapter Four
## The Buck Starts Here

credit card with a Visa or MasterCard logo that you can use worldwide.

The catch is that, by law, you are supposed to report all this to the IRS. However, failure to do so is very hard to prove. After all, why should the government be allowed to invade your financial privacy?

The subject of foreign investing isn't brain surgery, but it's not a rerun of *Married with Children* either. It takes average intelligence to understand. I am going to cover some basics, then refer you to other sources for further study.

The first thing to consider is which country to use. After looking into the options I believe Switzerland is the best choice. The country is stable, its financial privacy laws are very strong, and it offers both good rates of interest as well as access to credit lines and other important services.

Over the years the U.S. government has tried to intimidate Switzerland into opening its banking records, but the country have stood firm against such efforts. In order for American investigators to seize your Swiss records they must first prove that you are guilty of a major crime, such as drug smuggling or terrorism. They must prove this to a Swiss court.

Accusations of tax evasion don't fly with the Swiss. They don't give a damn how much you cheat Uncle Sam. You can pay a middleman to open the account for you (costs from $100 to $300).

You can deal with the bank itself and save the cost. Accounts can be opened with a modest deposit, and usually no minimum balance is required. Customer service is excellent.

Do a search online for "opening Swiss bank account" and you will find tons of sites. I have no way of recommending one over another. Austria and Luxembourg offer similar opportunities to Sweden.

A lot of people think of opening a bank account in Canada. Personally I think this is a bad idea. Not only are Canadian privacy laws weaker than Sweden's, but there are concerns over Canada's long term stability. If Quebec ever votes to secede there may be a civil war. At the very least economic chaos will follow. In addition the Canadian foreign debt is many times that of the U.S. on a proportional basis. Were I you I would stay away from the Canucks.

The Cayman Islands have traditionally been a popular tax haven, but the U.S. has become increasingly aggressive towards its government lately, demanding to see the accounts of American citizens. As a result there is no reasonable expectation of privacy if you bank there. Other Caribbean nations should be avoided for the same reason.

You need to learn more about this option before you take it. Fortunately there are plenty of good books on the subject. I recommend Trent Sands' fine volume *Personal Privacy Through Foreign Investing* from Loompanics as a good starting point.

If foreign banking isn't your cup of tea, then you might want to look at investing in...

## Collectibles

People get excited by the strangest things. I have met folks who prize old bottles, glassware and sewing machines and maintain extensive collections of them. Antiques, comic books, baseball cards, dolls, buttons, rocks, knick knacks, toys, tea kettles, thimbles and countless other things have their fans as well.

I myself am a fan of the old Universal monster movies. I own all sorts of things related to them, like posters of the Frankenstein monster and plastic models of Dracula and the Wolf Man. The human urge to collect is powerful indeed.

This can be good news for you. At the same time it can be a road to disaster if you are careless, impulsive or stupid. Investing in collectibles requires caution and savvy to be profitable.

## Chapter Four
## The Buck Starts Here

Remember the Ty Beanie Baby craze a few years ago? Folks were paying thousands of dollars for floppy little cloth toys. Whole shopping channels were devoted to selling them. Magazines wrote in detail about each new one that came out. People who should have known better spent real money on these things, hoping to sell them later for big profits. Companies other than Ty produced their own rip off versions.

Then overnight the bottom fell out. Now you can buy Beanie Babies for a quarter that once would have sold for hundreds of dollars. Plenty of people lost big bucks "investing" in a stupid fad.

This is a classic example of the "bubble effect." Something new comes along and is tagged as a "sure way" to make big bucks, making people want to get in on the "ground floor." Talk of the item's value becomes self-fulfilling prophecy, as demand sends the asking price through the ceiling. People buy huge quantities, speculating that it will be worth big bucks at a future time.

Unfortunately the actual value of the item never reaches expectations. Once this is realized the bubble bursts, and its price falls through the floor, ruining people who sank money into it. The same thing happened with the Internet stock craze of the 1990s.

Having said this, I should also point out that fortunes have been made buying and selling collectible items. One of the keys is to invest in things that have an extensive and well-established network of enthusiasts. A classic example is antiques. There are millions of Americans who love old furniture, books, etc. Someone wise in the ways of this business can do very well buying and selling.

Comic books and baseball cards are old standbys as well. The interest in these products is only going to grow as time goes on. A person who owns a copy of *Action Comics* number one from June of 1938 is literally sitting on two hundred thousand dollars or more. It contains the first appearance of Superman. It originally sold for a dime.

Copies of *Detective Comics* number one, where Batman first appeared, have disappointing values by comparison. In good shape they go for only a hundred grand. It too sold for ten cents when it came out.

A thorough knowledge of the collectibles you want to invest in is essential. PBS has programs like *The Antique Roadshow*. They can be a good starting point. *How to Make $20,000 a Year in Antiques and Collectibles Without Leaving Your Job*, by Bruce Johnson, is a well-regarded guide. You can get it from Amazon.com or order it from any bookstore. It's possible that the book in your hands right now will one day be worth millions, once the author becomes world famous as an economic scholar and barbecue chef. But I wouldn't bet on it.

While we're on this subject, we should talk a little about…

## The Precious Metals

In survivalist circles there has long been an enthusiasm for using these as a primary investment vehicle, based on fear of the inevitable "crash" that's always just around the corner. Gold, in particular, is recommended. "After all," they say, "no one ever said that gold isn't worth the paper it's printed on."

Previously in this book I have illustrated points by using self-deprecating anecdotes. I shall do so again now. In the early 1990s I stumbled across a book entitled *Bankruptcy 1995*, by Harry Figgie. In it he predicted that the American economy would collapse halfway through the 1990s, due to the crushing federal deficit.

His arguments were impressive. He used lots of economic terms and plenty of charts to prove his points. By the end of the book I was convinced that Armageddon was just around the corner. In preparation I started buying up silver coins and stashing them away. That way when the dollar was worthless I

## Chapter Four
## *The Buck Starts Here*

would have something of "real" value to barter with, unlike the foolish ones who were putting their money into stocks.

Well, 1995 came and went. The economy didn't collapse, the stock market went through the roof, and my silver coins actually lost value. I finally sold them at a 20% loss and bought U.S. savings bonds instead. As for Figgie's book you can buy a copy at Amazon.com. At the time of this writing they start at a penny.

The point of this sad story is that *precious metals suck as a primary investment*. Now before you sell those gold coins you've held onto all these years let me clarify what I am saying. Although gold, silver, platinum, etc. are poor vehicles for investment, they are excellent forms of economic insurance.

Allow me to explain. If Figgie's nightmare scenario had come true then my silver coins would have indeed been worth a fortune. That's because these metals historically go the opposite direction of more traditional investments. When times are good their values go down. But when inflation and unemployment rear their ugly heads they go up.

The reason for this is basic human psychology. When people's jobs are secure and their paychecks fat they feel confident. They proclaim their nation and their president the greatest in the world. And they invest in their economic system by buying stock in companies and bonds from their government.

However, when recession comes and wages fall the public loses faith in the system. The president becomes "that SOB" and the nation is seen as going down the wrong path. People start looking for things with "real" value that have stood the test of time. And what has been held in esteem by more people through the ages than gold and silver? So they gravitate towards the metals as a surefire way of protecting their wealth.

With this in mind you can see why gold, silver, and possibly platinum should be part of your investment plan. If all else ever really does go to Hell then you will still have something of value. Think of it as financial insurance.

Keep in mind that I am not a financial planner nor an advisor by trade. But, were I to advise someone how to structure an investment plan for funds earned in the underground economy it would look something like this:

Taking a given amount, say ten thousand dollars:
- 50% would go into an interest bearing Swiss bank account.
- Another 30% would go into carefully chosen collectibles, purchased anonymously with cash.
- Finally, 20% would go into gold and silver coins, bought anonymously and kept well hidden.

Such a plan offers security along with the potential for solid growth. It is also easy to conceal from prying eyes. This adds the advantage of privacy.

There is one other form of investing we should discuss.

## The Alpha Strategy

*The Alpha Strategy* is the name of a book by John Pugsley. Though currently out of print, numerous used copies are available through online booksellers like Amazon.com. I read this book in the early 1990s. Unlike the one by Figgie I have never regretted doing so.

The first half of the book is devoted to a discussion of economics and investments, but it is the second half that is relevant to our discussion here. In it the author advises his readers to bypass saving money for a rainy day. Instead he encourages them to buy goods that they need for daily living in quantity, and to set these aside for the future.

To illustrate: let's say I'm worried that my job may end in a few months. Conventional wisdom says to squirrel away cash now, so that when the time comes I'll still be able to buy groceries, clothes, personal items, etc. Pugsley says that to do so

## Chapter Four
## The Buck Starts Here

will expose my savings to the ravages of inflation, the possibility of currency devaluation, etc.

In order to bypass this I should simply buy the things I know I will need to sustain myself during a jobless period. For example, I should stuff my pantry with food, my closet with extra clothes, and my garage with medicines, shampoo, towels, soap, etc. When the time of crisis does come I will be well prepared for it, for I will have saved up *real* wealth, not pictures of dead presidents with no intrinsic value.

This book was written in the 1970s during a period of hyper-inflation, when the goods were rising to a greater value than that of cash. In such times a plan like the Alpha Strategy makes good sense. Buying a case of paper towels today ensures that you don't pay twice as much for them a year from now.

The plan makes less sense during periods of low inflation, such as we have enjoyed for the last 20 years or so. Nonetheless, it's hard to argue with the wisdom of having an emergency or survival pantry stuffed with things you'll need to ride out an emergency or sustained crisis.

For those interested in pursuing this concept further, I recommend the book *Don't Get Caught with Your Pantry Down*, by James Stevens. *How to Develop a Low Cost Family Food Storage System* and *Survivalist's Medicine Chest* are also good resources. They are available from the publisher of this book.

### A Lesson from John Gotti

This book is about making money with legitimate goods and services. The world of drug dealing, prostitution, etc., is outside its scope. Nonetheless, the story of this late mobster's downfall contains valuable lessons for anyone interested in tax-free profits.

## Under the Table and Into Your Pocket
The How and Why of the Underground Economy

Gotti ruled the New York Gambino crime family from the mid-80s to the early 90s. After successfully engineering the murder of his boss, Paul Castellano, on December 16, 1985, he took over as kingpin. Suddenly he was in control of nearly unlimited wealth and power.

Unlike his reclusive predecessor, Gotti enjoyed the public eye. He was often seen wearing lavishly expensive suits, riding in big cars and dining at expensive restaurants. He became something of a celebrity in the public's eyes. The media christened him "the Dapper Don."

The New York Attorney's Office soon set their sights on him, and beginning in 1986 they brought him to trial three times. Each time he was acquitted. Soon Gotti became known as "the Teflon Don," a reference to the fact that no charges seemed to stick to him.

Gotti was ultimately brought down by his refusal to keep a low profile. He was perceived as totally unafraid of the authorities, mocking them with his casual spending of large sums, his outward show of wealth and his frequent public appearances. The government decided that such open defiance of its authority could not be tolerated.

Enter the FBI. As powerful as the Mob was, it could not outspend or outfight the most powerful, the best financed and most ruthless law enforcement agency in history. It spent millions of dollars and invested countless man hours in bringing down the Dapper Don.

Finally in 1992 they scored a conviction for murder and racketeering against him and sent him to prison. He died of cancer ten years later.

The lesson for us is that defying the law is one thing, making a spectacle of it is another. Secretly enjoying a few amenities like big screen TVs and hot tubs carries little danger. Dressing in five thousand dollar suits when you have no legal

## Chapter Four
## The Buck Starts Here

means of support is quite risky. Keep your head low and your pleasures discreet and you should be okay.

Some luxury goods are easier to conceal than others. Nice TVs and stereos can be enjoyed in the privacy of one's basement rec room. A trip to a nice hotel or resort away from one's residence can be enjoyed without worry so long as cash is used. Conversely, flashy jewelry advertises wealth like nothing else. A giant home owned by a janitor screams "Crook!" A high dollar auto can get you labeled as a drug dealer if your official job title is convenience store clerk.

Closely tied to this is another rule you dare not break: **KEEP YOUR MOUTH SHUT.** Don't tell anyone about the underground nature of your business. If a customer asks why you want cash tell them it avoids the hassle of bounced checks. Offer them a discount for paying you in greenbacks.

And remember that Hell hath no fury like a spouse scorned. That loving partner could one day be a bitter enemy. Anything you tell him or her now might give them the means to ruin you later on. Make sure that you are totally devoted to each other and that they are worthy of complete trust.

# Chapter Five
# Case Histories

## What about benefits?

Okay, we've studied some basics and reviewed the different levels of the underground economy. Now let's look at some people who have actually made money in it. The names and certain details have been changed, but the methods each of them used can be applied to your situation as well.

### Patty, the Doll Maker

Patty is a 43-year-old housewife who is home most of the time. She was injured in a work-related accident five years ago and cannot hold a regular job due to back problems. She draws a small monthly stipend from the legal settlement she won against the company. Her husband is a construction worker, and his income alone is insufficient to support both them and their eight-year-old son, Todd.

She is a hard worker by nature and has found a way to supplement the family's income. She has nurtured a love of sewing all her life, and also has an extensive collection of dolls. One day she decides to combine her interests and start hand-making them for resale.

She starts by picking up a doll collector's magazine to see what styles are popular. She then buys patterns at a local fabric store along with crafts and other supplies and sets to work. Her first efforts resemble mutated freaks more than cute little

## Under the Table and Into Your Pocket
### The How and Why of the Underground Economy

people, but she keeps at it. Soon she is making soft, cuddly, adorable little toys that any girl would love.

There is a flea market near her home that draws over a thousand visitors a weekend, and she plans to sell her creations there. It is late winter, and she works hard to finish a full two dozen dolls before Easter weekend, when she will open her business. She researches the going price for similar dolls, and prices hers 10-20% below what they go for in retail shops. She dresses them in bright spring colors, and even fashions hats and shoes for them.

She goes to the market the weekend before Easter to scout it out and to pay her table rent. Twenty bucks gets her two adjoining tables three feet wide and eight feet long. They are located near the snack bar, the busiest part of the market.

The next few days are busy ones as she finishes her dolls. She also makes some signs advertising her booth, which she will hang up at the entrance to the market. The owner allows the dealers to do this.

The tables at the market are bare wood, so she buys some second-hand blankets to cover them with. They are also outdoors, so she breaks out their old beach umbrella to give her shade from the sun. She buys some nice shopping bags for a few pennies apiece from a variety store, makes sure she has plenty of change for customers, and sets aside a chair to sit in and a portable radio to listen to.

The night before the sale her husband loads his pickup truck with her dolls and other supplies, and they arrive at the market at 7 a.m. By 7:30 they have everything set up. Customers start to trickle by, but for the first couple of hours few show interest. Then a little girl spots the dolls and her eyes open wide. "Mommy, look!" she cries, grabbing her mother's hand and dragging her over to Patty's tables. A couple of minutes later she makes her first sale, which nets her a profit of ten dollars. Her husband gives her a big smile as she pockets the money.

## Chapter Five
## Case Histories

By day's end she has sold three dolls and netted thirty dollars profit. She looks around at her unsold stock, feeling discouraged. She had hoped to sell out! For a moment she considers not going back the next day, but the table is paid for and the fee is non-refundable. Tired, she and her husband pack the truck up and get home about four.

The next day they are at the market a little after seven. They take a little more time and care setting up the display this time, and Patty looks it over carefully to make sure it's attractive. About half an hour later an older woman stops, falls in love with the dolls, and buys three to give her granddaughters for presents. Patty is ecstatic. She has already earned as much money as she did the entire previous day.

Traffic slows to a crawl until about one, when the after church crowd hits the market. Parents bring their kids, and several little girls stop to look at Patty's table. Two of them persuade their parents to buy them a doll.

Then at three o'clock a large family walks by. The mother and three of her daughters fall in love with Patty's creations. "These are beautiful!" the mom says. Her kids agree. Then the mother frowns. "Kinda pricey though," she says, looking at the tags.

Patty sees a sale slipping away, but holds her ground. After a bit of haggling she agrees to give the woman a ten percent discount if she buys at least four dolls. She does, and Patty pockets thirty six dollars in profit after the exchange.

This is her last sale of the day, but she is quite happy. After figuring in the cost of their gas and lunch Patty and her husband figure that she netted ninety dollars in profit for the weekend. Though hardly a fortune, it's enough to buy gas and some of their groceries for the week.

Patty is now a regular at the flea market. After several weekends she moved from her outside tables to a spot in the building. It costs her thirty dollars for two days but the foot traffic is greater, so it evens out. Sometimes sales are good, sometimes bad. Christmas is her best time of year; she can make as much as two hundred dollars in a weekend.

On average she nets a little over a hundred dollars a week from the business, enough to help cover the bills and even allow the family an occasional treat, like a nice dinner out. Patty is proud of herself, and likes making money off of something she enjoys doing. She and her family are making it, without a penny in "help" from Uncle Sam.

### Glenn, the Graphic Artist

Glenn Strange is a graphic artist who lives in a middle-class subdivision in Atlanta, Georgia. His wife is a pediatric nurse, and together the two of them earn a good income. But they also have two kids and a great deal of credit card debt, so money is tight most of the time.

Glenn is interested in supplementing his income, and he decides that a resume preparation service would be a good sideline. So he buys a book on starting a small business and starts to read it. At first he figures that working for himself will be easy. After all, skilled resume preparers are in high demand, and his writing and design skills are excellent.

Then he begins to learn how much red tape is involved in starting a business. There is the license from the city, then the tax ID number from the state. Also he must file quarterly taxes on his earnings.

He leaps through one hurdle after another, and then makes a major mistake: he mentions his plans to his neighbor. Two days later he receives an injunction in the mail. It seems that his homeowners association has a rule against home-based businesses, and the board has taken out a restraining order against him. His only choice is to rent an office for his part time work.

## Chapter Five
## Case Histories

Sitting at home one night crunching the numbers, he buries his head in his hands. In despair he realizes that, after paying for all the licenses, fees, taxes, and office rent his plan is too saddled with expense to ever turn a profit. He decides to give up.

Glenn's problem is that he has lived his entire life kowtowing to the system; the merest thought of defying it in any way never crosses his mind. His wife, however, is not so timid. She is a libertarian and a reader of unusual and controversial books. She shows him one entitled, **Under the Table and Into Your Pocket**. "Darling, you ought to read this. I think it will help you," she offers.

He eyes it suspiciously. "Isn't the author that nut who writes about building catapults and hiding out from your creditors?" "Yes, that's him!" she says brightly. She then persuades him to read the book.

As Glenn reads the book the wool is pulled from his eyes, and he realizes that he has surrendered control of his life to the government and to his housing board. "To Hell with them!" he cries out in righteous fury. "I'm gonna do it without their permission!"

A week later he takes out an ad in his local shopping paper for his resume service. It lists his name, his e-mail address and his phone number. He runs the ad for a month. The first two weeks he hears nothing.

During the third one he gets an e-mail from an engineer who wants a resume prepared. He calls the guy; they meet at a local coffee shop, and a deal is struck with a handshake. Three days later the engineer gets his resume and Glenn gets a check for his services, which he cashes at his customer's bank.

The next week he receives three voice mails and an e-mail from potential clients. He meets each in a coffee house or restaurant, shows them samples of his design work, and strikes

## Under the Table and Into Your Pocket
The How and Why of the Underground Economy

deals with three of them. Within a week he is almost two hundred dollars richer.

As time goes on he gets more and more assignments. Eventually he stops advertising in the shopper, as word of mouth alone is giving him as much work as he can handle.

His side work attracts no attention, as he does it on his home computer. Supply costs are minimal. He even hears his asshole boss at his regular job wondering why they don't get any resume jobs anymore. Glenn smiles and sips his coffee.

He is discrete with his earnings, keeping them in cash form and well-hidden in a fireproof safe. He pulls out money as he needs it, buying clothes for his kids, giving his wife extra spending money, and paying a little extra on his credit cards every month. He keeps the same house and the same car.

His snoopy neighbor notices his increased prosperity, but has no idea what the source of it is. "I got a raise" is Glenn's standard answer to those who notice he is doing well.

His wife knows his secret, of course, as it is impossible to hide. He thanks her regularly for showing him the book that started it all. "Thank God for Bill Wilson!" he is frequently heard to say. And thank God for the underground economy!

### The Man Who Loved Montana

Joe Berkeley has spent his entire life in New York City, dodging the muggers, fighting the traffic and living in fear. One year he takes a trip out west, where he experiences the awesome beauty of Montana. As he stands on the porch of his rented cabin he watches the sunset behind the Rocky Mountains, which reach towards heaven and stretch north to south as far as the eye can see. "I'm going to move here," he vows to himself, as an eagle soars overhead in the vast, cloudless blue sky that is turning slowly to twilight.

Then reality hits. Joe is an urban planner by trade, a vocation for which there is little demand in Big Sky Country. He

## Chapter Five
## Case Histories

looks at telecommuting, but finds it is impossible. Dozens of resumes sent across the state yield nothing.

Then one day Joe looks out the window of his cramped apartment at the endless skyscrapers, the filthy street and the nasty people of the Big Apple. "I've gotta get out of here somehow," he tells himself. "This city is Hell."

So Joe quits his job, empties his bank account, trades in his Saab for a Ford F-350 pickup and starts driving west. He rents a condo in Missoula and starts looking for work. He is confident he will find something.

Six months later he is nearly broke, very hungry, and desperate. Then he notices his neighbor is moving. She has found a starter home a few miles away.

She drives a small economy car, and is struggling to fit her belongings into it. He goes over to talk to her and see if he can help. "I'd appreciate a hand," she says. "I can't afford a moving truck and none of my friends could get the day off to help me."

Joe offers his truck and his two hands, and together they get the job done in a few hours. "Thanks so much!" she says when they are done, after giving him a big hug. "I wish there were more like you around. It's impossible to find anyone dependable to help you move!"

Her words light a spark in Joe's mind. A few days later he is browsing through a used bookstore when he spots a book entitled, *How to Make $15 to $50 an Hour With a Pickup Truck or Van*. He buys it. It is all about a guy who lived in a small town where jobs were scarce. He found he could make good money helping people move, as well as hauling away their junk for them.

Joe follows his advice. He takes out ads in a local paper, puts up fliers on bulletin boards, and even puts a sign on his truck door. He gets a cell phone and lists its number on the ads. He soon gets a call from a man who needs some brush hauled away and a garage cleaned out.

Joe sets up the job, shows up when he is supposed to and does more than he was asked. The customer is delighted and pays him in cash, as he requests. "I've got a cousin across town who needs a storage building cleaned out," he tells Joe. "I'm gonna give him your number."

The cousin calls him the next day. He offers Joe $100 to clean out the building. "Do what you want to with the stuff," he directs him. "It's nothing but old junk." Joe goes through it anyway, and to his delight discovers some old comic books worth nearly 200 bucks! He sells these at a local shop in addition to getting his fee from the cousin.

Work comes in at a slow but steady pace from his ads plus personal referrals. Joe finds so much valuable stuff in the so-called "junk" he's paid to throw away that he earns almost as much from it as from his fees for hauling.

Then he gets another idea. He goes down to the nearest Home Depot and buys a snow blower and chain saw. He offers to cut down damaged or unwanted trees as well as clear walkways, drives, etc., with the snow blower. He cuts the trees up and sells the pieces as firewood.

Soon Joe is doing well financially. In addition his health has improved from all the hard work, and he is much happier living in Montana than the Rotten Apple. All in all his life has improved drastically from both his relocation and his underground business.

There is one thing, he lacks, though: the companionship of the opposite sex. One day he is walking through the grocery store when he sees the woman he helped move months before. They fall into a conversation which leads to him asking her out.

Over dinner that night he tells her about how his life has turned around. By the end of the evening the pair has devel-

## Chapter Five
## Case Histories

oped feelings for each other, and romance soon follows. Another happy ending thanks to the underground economy!

The above stories are based on the real life experiences of those who have worked tax-free. As you can see the underground economy offers numerous opportunities for both profit and freedom. And you can be part of it.

In the rest of this chapter we'll look at specific ways to make money under the table. Each of the enterprises discussed can be gotten into for little or no money. They can be worked while keeping a low profile. And each is potentially lucrative. You may find the ideal business for you in the following pages.

At the very least you'll get ideas that can lead to profitable self-employment. So read on, and learn all about yard work, small engine repair, peddling, selling your body (legally), panhandling, and other great business opportunities. The best is yet to come.

### Lawn Care

There's money in grass — and I don't mean the kind you smoke. Americans love their lawns. And as their lives grow more hectic they have less time to work on them. In addition the teens that used to dominate this biz are all inside numbing their brains with video games. All this creates enormous opportunities for you, o aspiring entrepreneur.

Starting costs can be as little as a few hundred bucks, less if you already have a mower. You can stick with push mowing small lawns, or get a riding mower and take on jobs of a half acre or more. You might want to get a bag attachment to collect the cuttings in, but it isn't strictly necessary.

A truck or van to haul your mower in is good, but you can get away with a car pulling a tow-behind trailer. Don't try to get away with cramming your stuff in your back seat though. You'll look an idiot.

This is good, honest, hard work. Your main challenge will be the heat. Make sure you can take it before jumping in. If you've ever seen guys who do this for a living you've probably noticed they're skinny and darkly tanned.

They also drink a lot of beer.

Earning a tax-free income is quite easy. Ads can be placed on bulletin boards at church or community centers, or even in supermarkets and post offices.

Deals with customers can be closed with a verbal agreement and a handshake. Cash and checks are the usual methods of payment. Remember: get the check made out to you and cash it at the customer's bank.

If you get into this gig and like it, then you can expand into related fields, like bush trimming, flower bed planting, fertilizing and weeding. Caution: there are ten million books on how to do this stuff and most of them aren't worth a damn. Learn the ropes by hanging out with an experienced landscaper or, even better, by working for one for a summer or two. Learn how he or she bills their clients. Try to set your rates lower when you strike out on your own.

You can run this one on any of the levels of the underground economy, including totally off the books, with little trouble. The important thing is to be reliable. There are a lot of drunks and losers in this business, so if you prove you can actually show up and do your thing you'll have all the work you can handle. Good luck!

## Small Engine Repair

If you're anything like me you enjoy mechanical stuff, including working on cars. However, it seems that the auto companies have been involved in a conspiracy over the last three decades to make vehicles increasingly complicated. It

## Chapter Five
## Case Histories

63

has gotten to the point that the "shade tree" mechanic can't do anything under the hood.

There is an alternative for those who want to make good money and still enjoy the smell of gas and oil, though. That is by working on small engine powered equipment. In the south this is primarily lawnmowers. In colder regions it can include snow blowers, snowmobiles, chain saws, and a host of other stuff.

The first thing you will need is a work area. Fortunately it need not be anything huge. A regular garage or even a shed can be plenty of room. Either a solid wood or concrete floor will do. It doesn't have to be immaculate, but for heaven's sake keep the dust down! It can get into engines and destroy them quick.

You will need to be able to have two or three large mowers in the shop at one time and others outside but kept out of the weather. One absolute must is good ventilation. Have plenty of windows and a fan blowing outwards.

As for tools, a good set of Craftsman or another quality brand should suffice, so long as you have both metric and standard ratchets and wrenches in all widely used sizes. Vise grips, metal clamps, and a few specialized tools like a multimeter and vacuum gauge will come in handy.

Though most people will bring their machines to you, it is helpful if you can pick it up at their residence on request. A truck, van, or pull-behind trailer is essential. You can hit them up for a pickup and delivery fee on top of the repair bill.

You will need some formal training unless you have years of experience. Fortunately the Foley-Belsaw Company offers an outstanding home study course in the field. Check them out at www.foley-belsaw.com. They'll send you a big envelope full of info.

The cost for the course is eight to nine hundred bucks, but they will let you pay for it by the month without even checking your credit. They will also help you with business signs, advice, ordering parts, etc. when the time comes. I have seen their materials and they are excellent. I cannot recommend this course enough for anyone wanting to do this kind of work.

As with lawn care, this gig can be done on any level of the underground economy. As it is potentially quite lucrative, you may want to go to the hassle of setting yourself up legally and just doing cash work on the side. That way you can expand into the big time with no problem. I know guys who started out small in this business and now have huge shops with several employees. *Warning:* your work will likely be heavy in the summer months and light in the winter. Be ready to pull some serious hours May through August or be prepared to turn down a lot of jobs.

## *Profile*

Joe S. is a retired metal shop worker who had to leave the mainstream working world early due to back trouble. He took a mail-order course in small engine work and set up a small shop in his garage. He has a business license and all the "legit" stuff, but it is well-known that he will cut you a break for a cash job.

Joe likes to hunt, camp, and fish, so he only works about twenty hours a week, mostly April through August. He makes good money in the early season doing tune-ups and oil changes. At that time folks are getting their mowers ready for the summer. He also buys up used machines, fixes them up and sells them. He runs ads in the local shopper, and also has three or four mowers in his front yard all the time with a "For Sale" sign in front of them.

Joe gets his parts from a local business. He limits himself to push mowers, as the riding ones are heavy and cumbersome and working on them aggravates his back. There is little heavy

Chapter Five
Case Histories

lifting involved in what he does and he can sit at the bench while doing the work. Joe brings in good money for his investment of time and enjoys his life.

## Computer Tutor

The damn things are everywhere, and you can't do anything without one anymore. I'm talking about personal computers. They popped up in the early 80's on desktops and in schools. The first ones were little more than glorified typewriters. Since then they have transformed the world as their capabilities have leapt forward at a dizzying pace.

The pace of progress is so fast that a lot of people, especially middle-aged and older folk, are scratching their heads in confusion. "What the devil is a 'mouse' and how can anything called 'RAM' be good," they want to know. If you are one of those who is tech savvy you can make a killing off of showing "dummies" how to surf the Web and use programs like Word.

As a computer tutor your investment will be nearly nothing, as you are selling the knowledge inside you head. Among the things you can do: advise customers on what kind of PC to get, show them how to set it up, get signed up with an ISP, and use e-mail. You can also teach them useful things like composing and printing letters, doing simple desktop publishing, and balancing their checkbooks.

You will, of course, need to know a lot about computers, but you won't have to worry about "A+ certification" or anything fancy like that. You may already know a great deal if you work with computers in your current job.

Microsoft and other software manufacturers offer various levels of certification for their products; you can find out about these by going to their web sites. Almost any bookstore will have a computer section with tons of volumes on learning computer skills. You can also check out your local community college; they usually offer lessons on how to use a PC.

You will need to be personable and patient, as your pupils will likely have lots of questions. In addition many of them will be nervous or even afraid of the equipment. Meet them on their level and take your time with them. Nobody likes the smug know-it-all type who treats others like idiots.

This gig can easily be worked on a cash basis, especially if you only work with individuals or small classes. If you get offered any corporate stuff, like teaching 30 people how to use Microsoft Excel, then you can pocket some serious bucks. You will need to be "legit" to score stuff like that, though. Computer tutors can make big bucks virtually anywhere in the U.S. as well as around the world. Give this one some serious thought. Below is a sample ad you can customize:

> **Has the Computer Age Got You Confused? I CAN HELP!**
> My name is Beverly Knowitall, and I am a certified computer nerd! If you need to learn how to buy one, how to get on the Web, or anything else, give me a call! **555-5555**

## Merchant

We touched on this a bit earlier when we discussed flea markets and street vendors. I want to revisit it now.

Few opportunities offer the kind of potential rewards you will find in selling products. Not only is your choice of products nearly unlimited, but so are the venues by which you can sell them and still earn a tidy tax-free income. You should choose to accept only cash payments. Personal checks can bounce.

Of all the options discussed in this book, this is the one I am most familiar with, so I'll spend some time talking about it. The most important decision by far is *what to sell*. This will be determined by whether you want to make your products or acquire them (I say "acquire" because there are legal alternatives

## Chapter Five
## Case Histories

to shelling out bucks to a merchandise wholesaler, which we'll discuss in a bit).

Artists, craft enthusiasts, hobbyists, wood workers, photographers, etc., can create their own goods. People love handmade furniture, jewelry, toys, pictures, etc. Someone skilled in making them can earn an income almost anywhere.

As for pricing, the best guide is what similar items are going for in your area. However, you must *price to sell*. I have seen local studios and galleries ask exorbitant prices for items that sit on their shelves year after year.

How they keep their doors open I'll never know. I can tell you this, though: the key to success in merchandising is a strong, steady flow of goods for cash. So make sure what you are asking is what a customer will actually pay.

You must know what will move in your area. Here in the south anything related to the Civil War is big, especially statuettes or paintings of Confederate soldiers. I doubt the demand is quite as strong in Hoboken, New Jersey. Visit a flea market or two and see what people are carrying in their hands.

Vanity items will sell *everywhere*. They include jewelry, tools, lingerie, makeup, perfumes/colognes, or anything that makes the person feel strong, pretty, or sexy. Bath oils, incense, and skin care products are in the same vein and usually do well.

If you have lost weight and can convince people it's because of something you sell then you can get rich. Have "before" and "after" pics of yourself without a shirt or wearing a bathing suit to back up your claims. Also have some literature on hand explaining the "scientific process" that makes your stuff work.

Collectibles are almost always a sure bet as well, but you must be into the items yourself to know what people want. Comic books and baseball cards are the old standbys. NASCAR items, swords and daggers, anything with a SF or fantasy theme, drug-related paraphernalia — all these have fans across the USA.

I mentioned before that there are alternatives to buying goods. One of the best ones is to combine your selling business with a clean up or moving one. A very wise man who lived in a college town used to put up signs all over campus offering to haul away unwanted stuff for free. At semester or year's end, he would walk off with a fortune in TVs, VCRs, computers, clothes, books, and sports equipment. He sold them out of his own store, and his sales were almost pure profit.

Dumpster diving is a way to score some premium stuff, but talk about a crapshoot! You may get TVs, electronics, CDs, stereos, all kinds of cool stuff. Then again you might find yourself buried in banana peels, moldy hamburger buns, and rats. If you want to explore this route, read *The Art and Science of Dumpster Diving* by John Hoffman, listed in the back of this book.

We talked a bit about setting up at flea markets before, so I'll skip that and talk about other ways to peddle your goods. If there is a vacant lot, closed-up gas station, or old strip mall with no active stores in your area then you have a spot rent free and ready to go. It's unlikely the cops will give you any grief. If they do then just say "Sorry, officer," pack up your stuff and scat.

A lot of neighborhoods forbid door-to-door salespeople, but you may live in a place where they're allowed. If so then you can load an old suitcase and start knocking on doors. Make sure you've got stuff that will move quickly, and be prepared to show how it works.

In the old days peddlers would just park their cars, set up a small card table with items from their trunk and sell right there. It's a lot harder to do this than it used to be; local store

## Chapter Five
## Case Histories

owners get pissed and bitch to the cops. If you're in a smaller town it may still be an option for you.

Some people have asked me about setting up an online store. This doesn't seem very conducive with the underground economy. It's nearly impossible to pay in cash, and electronic transactions leave tons of trails right to you. Those wishing to make tax-free cash should avoid selling on the Net.

Jordan L. Cooper is an old flea market veteran who has written several books on making money buying and selling. In addition to the one recommended earlier, the book *Shadow Merchants: Successful Retailing Without A Storefront* is a must read for those looking at this business (also listed in the back of this book).

Buying from auctions for resale is an art unto itself. In the appendix you will find an article which discusses it in depth. It was written by me and appeared in an issue of *Backwoods Home Magazine*. Feel free to use the ideas it presents.

### Booze Provider

Ivy is an African-American woman in her 40's who lives in a mobile home park in South Carolina. Most of her neighbors are white rednecks, but contrary to stereotype they harbor little or no racial prejudice. She lives quietly and safely among them.

In fact she gets lots of visits from them on Sundays. That's because local ordinances forbid selling alcohol on the Sabbath (this is common throughout the Southeast). On Saturdays Ivy puts her Sam's Club warehouse membership to good use. She stocks up on beer and cigarettes, though she neither smokes nor drinks.

A lot of her neighbors start getting a powerful thirst for a brew early Sunday afternoon and have already exhausted the supply they bought Friday when they got their paycheck cashed. So they visit Ivy. She sells them a can or bottle of their favorite brew at about twice what she paid for it. The rednecks don't complain. They're glad to have a source for alcohol on the Lord's Day.

Many of her neighbors are tobacco addicts who have lost their drivers licenses due to repeated DUIs. When the craving for a cancer stick hits they too go to see Ivy. She sells them smokes a stick, a pack or a carton at a time, again at twice what she paid. The grateful addicts cheerfully fork over their change and walk away happy.

Ivy has been doing this for a number of years. Though not strictly legal it's nothing the local cops care to do anything about. She has squirreled away almost ten grand in cash over the last four years from her sideline, enough to cover her daughter's tuition and other expenses at the local community college for two years. The young lady plans to become an accountant.

## Handyman

My brother is the proverbial Jack-of-all-Trades. He can do plumbing, electrical, automotive, and carpentry work to a fair degree. He's built computers, grown award-winning tomatoes and operated all kinds of tractors and heavy equipment. Though not a master of any one trade he has a fairly in depth knowledge of at least a dozen.

Speaking hypothetically, of course, someone like him could do very well in the underground economy as a handyman. People everywhere need all sorts of odd jobs done. Drywall needs patching, electrical outlets need installing, oil needs changing, scissors need sharpening, flowers need planting, vinyl seats need mending, pipes need unclogging, etc., etc., etc.

All of these jobs require a moderate knowledge of many different trades, but none require a master of them. Hence, the handyman or handywoman. He or she may clean carpet one day, move furniture the next, haul stuff to the city dump the

*Chapter Five
Case Histories*

day after that, then finish up the week building a chicken coop or a storage shed. The work can be hard, but there is variety to it, and good money can be made, in cash with no questions asked. You can start out by advertising as for the yard work gig, but once you get rolling word of mouth should keep you going strong.

The biggest thing that trips people up in this gig is biting off more than you can chew. Before taking a job be sure you can handle it. If you screw up someone's wiring or plumbing you can land in hot water really quick. If limited in your abilities you might want to stick to manual labor stuff like hauling garbage, clearing brush and simpler stuff like painting. You'll still stay busy, but your back will be sore as hell for a while.

If you want to know more about this option, then check out *The Handyman's Handbook : The Complete Guide to Starting and Running a Successful Business,* by David Koenigsberg. You can get it at Loompanics Unlimited or by order from any bookstore. The author works in the field himself, so all his advice is real world stuff, not "I researched it really good" BS.

## Janitor/House Cleaner

Clean up this dump, will ya? It looks like crap. What's that? You're too lazy to do it? Then hire someone, or better yet do the work yourself anyway. Then start your own underground business taking care of other's messes.

Janitorial work has to be the ultimate "safe" job. They might move the factories to China, they may downsize all the office workers, but someone's always going to be needed to vacuum the floor, scrub the urinals and take out the trash. That could be you. And the money's better than you might think.

The easiest tax-free work to get is cleaning private homes. Women thrive doing this gig. Some of them provide their own cleaning supplies; others use the homeowners'. Even if you buy your own stuff you can get into this field for under two

## Under the Table and Into Your Pocket
The How and Why of the Underground Economy

hundred dollars, or for less than a hundred if you pick up a used vacuum and buy off-brand chemicals.

Word-of-mouth seems to be the best way to get customers. If you are a member of a church or a civic or community group then you likely already have a host of potential clients. Spread the word around that you want to make money cleaning and chances are you'll land assignments right away. It's a sign of our times that people will gladly pay others to do something they could easily do themselves.

Before you take on a job make sure that you and the client know exactly what is expected. I worked as a janitor in a textile plant throughout college and sometimes the expectations on me were absurd. For instance, a guy would show up drunk for third shift and puke all over the men's room. I would get the heat for it the next day, even though it happened hours after I had gone home.

Make a checklist of each thing you are getting paid to do, and have the client sign it. Then do it all to the best of your ability. Remember that people are picky as hell. It's worth pulling the sofa away from the couch to vacuum against the wall or dusting the top of the ceiling fan if it means making someone happy. You can then use them as a reference for landing more work.

Men have a tough time getting house cleaning work, but they can make it in the business by landing office gigs. Again word-of-mouth is the way to go. Find someone in your church or your lodge that owns a small business, say a construction company, or maybe the president of a local bank branch or a store owner. Then offer to come in two or three times a week to vacuum, mop, wipe down the counters and take out the trash. As with the house gigs make sure both sides know what is to be done. Do it right, and call your client every now and then to make sure they're satisfied. Nothing creates success in business like a core group of happy customers.

## Chapter Five
## Case Histories

Cleaning carpets or stripping and rewaxing floors are good ways to up your income. They're not hard to do, especially in smaller areas, say a hundred square feet or less.

You can get a free education in floor care by going to your local Oreck vacuum cleaner store. Ask the guy to show you how the "Orbiter" works. It's a pint-sized version of the monster floor buffers used in institutions.

He'll show you how it can clean carpets and also redo the finish on tile and linoleum. Then buy one from him; they run about three hundred bucks. Chemicals will set you back another hundred or so.

This gig is ideal for the underground economy. However it can become lucrative, especially if you get the chance to clean factories, large office complexes, or medical clinics. Then you need to start looking at going legit.

Yes, I'm going to recommend further reading for those interested in these options. The all time guru of cleaning is a fellow named Don Aslett, a self-made millionaire who earned his fortune with his janitorial firm. Get ahold of his book *Cleaning Up For A Living* (also available from Loompanics Unlimited). It'll give you all the dope, including how to price your work.

### Boarding House

Everybody needs shelter, and those who can rent it to others have a fantastic chance to earn casual income. Running a conventional apartment building would be beyond the means of the underground entrepreneur, but boarding houses and small trailer parks can easily be run on a cash basis. We'll look at both options.

Boarding houses used to be very common across the United States. They are much less so now, but can still be found. For underground economy purposes we'll assume that you own a

## Under the Table and Into Your Pocket
The How and Why of the Underground Economy

home with one or more spare bedrooms. Making extra cash with it is easy.

Put an ad in the local shopper or at your post office or market saying that you have a room for rent. Or even better rely on word of mouth through your church, regular job or circle of friends. You'll likely get better tenants that way. Being in a college town can help, as students are always looking for cheap housing. But you'll have to get used to losing your boarders during the summer months.

In the ad, list the rent you are asking. This can vary widely; I've seen rooms go for anywhere from a hundred bucks a month to the same for a week. If in doubt, price high then reduce it until you get takers.

In the old days the landlord or lady would include meals and even laundry service. This was the arrangement Sherlock Holmes and Dr. Watson enjoyed in their lodgings at 221-B Baker Street in London. I would advise not offering such perks in our modern era; the room is enough.

You should make sure it is furnished with a bed, mirror and dresser. A desk and chair are nice touches. Use leftover stuff from your garage or buy the furnishings cheap at the local thrift store. You also want to make sure the tenant or tenants have their own bathroom and kitchen. I suggest providing cable TV access and a small color television if you want to keep them quiet. There's no better tranquilizer than the tube, as prison wardens across the country can attest to.

The key to this gig is picking quality renters. You don't want any escaped fugitives or serial killers living under your roof. Requiring references and a deposit will go a long way towards screening out the riffraff. Look at the car they drive. Is it clean and in good repair? Do they use proper English, or is their talk peppered with slurred words and ghetto talk? Do they have a bumper sticker that says TO REPORT MY

## Chapter Five
## Case Histories

DRIVING CALL 1-800-EAT-SHIT or I'M THE ONLY HELL MY MOMMA EVER RAISED? Bad sign!

Do they work? If so, where and for how long? Can you call the employer to verify what they say? Do they have proper ID? Do they have kids? Is there a crazy ex-spouse trying to track them down? Are they willing to let you run a criminal records check on them?

You may also ask for a credit report, but in my opinion that's going too far. Plenty of decent folks have had trouble paying their bills in the past but have since gotten their act together. Better signs of a good renter are stable work history, a clean appearance and a respectful attitude.

Find out how often they get paid and expect the rent on each of their paydays. For example, if they get paid every Friday tell them you expect a week's rent that same day before five o'clock. Get your money before they burn through it, and have a cash only policy.

I advise not allowing drugs, alcohol or visits from the opposite sex. If your potential renter is attractive you may be tempted to trade lodging for an occasional roll in the hay. But thinking with your hormones can get you in trouble quick.

Being a landlord isn't for everyone. You've got to be ready to lean on a tenant if they don't respect the property or fail the pay the rent on a timely basis. Fail to rent to a minority or handicapped person and you might get sued. The best way to avoid this is to get tenants through word of mouth instead of running an ad.

If you do advertise, pay a local attorney a couple hundred bucks for an hour of his time and discuss your local housing laws with him or her. It's worth the cost and you'll easily recoup it when you start renting.

Pets can be a hassle. I would never let anyone keep a dog in their room, but a clean, neat cat or small animals like fish or a bird might work out. Sometimes renters get pissed and trash the room before leaving you in the lurch. Then you have to clean and repair the mess. Handyman skills can be very useful in this situation. You'll want to keep your business very low key if there are local codes or ordinances against lodging people.

I have lived in boarding houses off and on and the following profile is based on my experiences with one.

## The Lonely Old Woman

I had just moved to South Carolina and needed a place to stay. I saw an ad in the local paper offering a room for rent. I called the number and met a nice older lady who lived alone. She was a semi-retired real estate agent and had a large bedroom she never used. We agreed on a price and I moved in.

I gave her some references, which she checked, and paid her a hundred bucks deposit and eighty five dollars for the first week's rent. I got bathroom and kitchen privileges. I was working nights at the time so I rarely saw her.

After a while I learned that she had been making money this way for years. Her last tenant was an older gentleman who had lived with her for quite a while. Their association ended when he failed to leave his room for a couple of days. She went in to check on him and saw him lying dead in the same bed I later slept in. He'd had a heart attack in his sleep.

In time she rented out another bedroom and a basement apartment and a little community formed in her home. We would prepare meals and watch TV together in her spacious living room. She brought in several hundred bucks a week tax-free from her little enterprise and having so many people around kept her from getting lonely. This was a very decent arrangement and lasted me for several months.

## Chapter Five
## Case Histories

## Trailer Park

The phrase conjures images of old cars up on blocks, drug dealers and hookers working out of their homes and scenes from the *COPS* TV show. With a few exceptions this pretty much sums up life in the average trailer park.

The flip side is that the owner of the park can make a ton of cash very quickly. For underground economy purposes you'll want to keep yours fairly small, no more than maybe a dozen trailers. You'll need a piece of land to put them on. A quarter to half an acre will do nicely, as you pack them in like sardines with just enough room for parking. In the South many people in rural areas have good-sized parcels of land and literally set up a park in their back yard.

You buy the units at auction for a thousand bucks or so apiece then move them onto your lot. They're generally shit holes that are falling apart, so you'll need to do some repairs, mostly replacing flooring and wiring. Don't make them fancy or nice, just livable. Do the minimum you have to in order to stay legal. Of course you'll need to have sewage, water, and electric lines run to each unit. You'll also need to provide mailboxes.

People who live in trailer parks range from college kids to senior citizens to criminals and other human debris. When I worked in credit and collections I used to visit them quite a bit. On Friday nights someone would always be playing their stereo so loud the ground shook. Their neighbors were usually too drunk to care.

How much the building inspector will poke his nose into your affairs varies widely. Here in Dixie I've seen parks that looked like a bomb was dropped on them and nobody cared. It helps to be a member of the First Baptist Church and drive a nice car. Then you're seen as a respectable businessman, not a slum lord.

## Under the Table and Into Your Pocket
The How and Why of the Underground Economy

A smart move is to make one of the tenants the "manager" in exchange for reduced rent. He or she should be able to deal with the tenants, collect their rent, and keep them relatively calm. Above all you want to avoid having the police show up a lot. That'll get you shut down quick.

As with the boarding house, take rent only in cash. I strongly suggest having your people pay weekly or bi-weekly, unless they are retirees. Trailer park types rarely have the discipline to put together a month's rent all at once.

Getting a hundred to two hundred bucks a week per trailer isn't hard. Do the math. If you're renting out, say, five trailers at one fifty a week that's $750.00 a week in cold hard cash. Expenses are minimal unless you have lots of maintenance problems, which is unlikely. I've seen parks where the duct work has fallen out the bottom of the trailers and there's no heat in winter. The residents know the landlord will never fix it, so when cold weather comes they set a kerosene heater in the middle of the living room and the whole family sleeps on the floor around it.

In the summer when it tops ninety-five degrees the trailers get as hot as Dante's inferno inside. But the tenants think they can't afford an air conditioner. So they sit outside and drink beer and smoke all day. If they crunched the numbers they'd realize they could buy an air conditioning window unit for what they spend a week on alcohol and cigarettes. I've never seen this actually happen.

There are ways to attract better clients. White trash types have usually screwed the local power utility in the past with unpaid bills and can't get an account in their name. So they try to find places that include electricity in the rent. If you insist they set up their own services you'll be eliminating the real bottom feeders. You can also rent only to seniors. Lots of older people are on tight incomes and will gladly move into

# Chapter Five
## Case Histories

the park if it's quiet and safe. You'll want to keep the units in pretty decent shape to attract good people to them.

An alternative is to rent out lots only and have the people bring in homes they own. Since they must have fairly good credit to buy their trailer you can get more stable people this way. They'll generally be working-class types but clean and decent. A lot of people don't realize that a person can be a redneck without being white trash. I've met lots of rednecks who were fine human beings, except for being dumb and kind of loud.

The following example is based on the experiences of a trailer park owner I knew in Georgia.

### An income for the retired years

Bob Morgan was a retired government worker who owned a nice home with ten acres. One day he went to an auction held by a local mobile home dealer and bought four units. He had them hauled to his land, where he had prepared lots for them. He and his wife went through them, cleaning them and doing repairs as necessary. Then he started to rent them out.

Bob took care of his units; they were clean, good little homes. He was very strict though. He had friends on the sheriff's department, and if a tenant was late with their rent, a deputy would be at their door the next day demanding that they pay up or vacate. This wasn't exactly legal (state law required the landlord to file papers and give the tenant thirty days notice) but the renters were dumb and the sheriff corrupt as hell.

Bob's rent included electricity, so he didn't let his boarders own air conditioners. Anyone who has ever spent a summer in Georgia knows what this meant.

Bob expected his rent on Friday afternoons and stayed home so the people could bring it over. He got a hundred and twenty bucks a week per unit. This was in the late 1980's, so if he's still around I'm sure he gets more now.

## Clergyperson/Marriage Minister

The United States is the most religious country in the western world. It also has very liberal laws regarding faith-based enterprises. For example, did you know that if you have a computer you can be a legally ordained minister in minutes? Simply go to the web site of the Universal Life Church (www.ulc.org) and fill out a very, very brief form. Don't worry if you're gay, female, or a mass murderer; the Universal Life Church invites everyone to join up. In seconds you'll be on their roster of ordained leaders. You can even print out a certificate attesting to your new status.

The Universal Life Church is a fun organization. It was started in 1959 by Kirby Hensley, a student of religion who rejected his Baptist upbringing and started his own church. From the beginning he insisted it have no creeds, no doctrines and no statements of faith. Members range from fervent Christians to practicing Buddhists and New Agers; even some atheists have joined up. The state of California tried to shut him down several times, but a strong victory in federal court has forever established his right to run his religion as he sees fit. It has also opened the door for hundreds of copycat "ministries" which do the same thing.

The church provides distance education in theology, psychology and metaphysics, and offers degrees in these subjects for a nominal fee. The coursework is not excessively arduous. Ordination entitles you to be called "reverend," but for an additional fee the church will send you a certificate proclaiming you to be a saint, prophet, apostle, guru, monsignor, abbot, thanatologist, nun, priest, or even a Universal Doctor of Absolute Reality!

## Chapter Five
## Case Histories

Reverend Hensley himself was openly anti-religious until his death in 1999, but respected the rights of his clergy to disagree with him. If your attitude towards faith is tolerant and laid back you'll love the Universal Life Church. It has ordained some 20 million people since its founding, including myself. After filling out the online application I got a popup from their homepage welcoming me to the fold. Hallelujah!

You may be wondering what the hell any of this has to do with the underground economy. The answer is that religion is the biggest moneymaker on earth, and ordination allows you to tap into the cash flow. The easiest way to do this is to set up a "marriage ministry." Millions of Americans get married every year. Many of them have no particular spiritual beliefs, but desire a church-type ceremony for sentimental reasons. This is where you come in. As an ordained minister (even one who got their credentials on the Internet) you can legally perform weddings anywhere in the United States. The Universal Life Church will sell you everything you need, including tons of information on how to do the ceremony, what to tell the couples, how to advertise your service and how much to charge.

Don't worry if you don't have a church building. A meeting hall can be rented and set up with folding chairs, flowers and a picture or two of Jesus for that heavenly touch. The couple pays for all this, of course. Those desiring a cheaper or simpler ceremony can be married outside, perhaps beneath an old oak tree, in a pastoral field, in the mountains or beside a waterfall or the ocean.

Where I live there are tons of services like this. The state of Tennessee, home of the Great Smoky Mountains National Park, supports them by making marriage licenses absurdly easy to get. Go to Pigeon Forge or Gatlinburg and see for yourself. The courthouse has annexes open on the weekend where you and your future spouse can be in and out in five minutes. Las Vegas offers similar opportunities.

Are you a bigamist? No worries. Tennessee doesn't require you to show a decree of divorce from your other spouse. Even if you do get caught bigamy is a misdemeanor in the state and only carries a thousand dollar fine.

Usually the minister and his wife work as a team. He does the vows and she takes pictures. These are developed and mailed to the bride and groom in a nice album. There are thousands of beautiful places in the national park as well as the Blue Ridge Parkway to hold the ceremony. Sometimes it's just the couple and the minister; other times dozens of people show up.

This is potentially very lucrative, but to stay under the IRS radar you want to keep things simple. Do mostly outside services and take a "love offering" in cash. If the couple wants an inside service let them pay for the building and have them make the arrangements separately from you.

In addition to marriage, people often seek a minister to perform a funeral for a loved one who had no religious affiliation. You can make arrangements with local mortuaries to have these people call you. Again, here your only role is to say a few words in exchange for a cash "gift." Handbooks for doing funerals can be bought from the Universal Life Church or at your local Christian bookstore.

It is difficult to say a bunch of kind words about someone you never met, so you don't want to offer a long and rousing speech about what a saint they were. After all, the dearly departed may have been a real SOB. Just follow the litany in the book, offer condolences to the guests, and take your money and go.

On rarer occasions you may be sought out to do baptisms, bless homes, or even do spiritual counseling. I advise steering clear of that last one as there are significant liability issues.

# Chapter Five
# Case Histories

Your counselee may blow his brains out after talking to you and all of the sudden the family smells lawsuit. Let the real clergy handle that kind of stuff. You're just in it for the money, right?

## *Brother Joe*

"I ain't got no diploma from no fancy Bible school, and I don't want one anyway," Brother Joe told me as we chatted in a restaurant. "I been reading the Good Book since I was a young'un and that's all the training anybody ever needed."

Brother Joe is sixty-years-old, chews tobacco and wears overalls except when he's marrying folks, at which times he breaks out a dark blue suit he's owned since the 1960's.

He was ordained through World Christianship Ministries (www.wcm.org), an organization similar to the Universal Life Church but somewhat stricter in its teachings. Candidates for ordination must claim to be Christians. "I looked at that other one" he says, referring to the ULC, "but I ain't no damn guru or swami; I'm just a preacher."

Brother Joe performs marriages for local people in eastern Tennessee. For fifty bucks he'll do the ceremony in the outside location of your choice or in a private home. His wife, a rather good photographer, takes pictures of the blessed event and puts them in an album for an additional fifty bucks. For fifty more she'll bake a nice cake for the occasion and set it up on a picnic table with paper plates and forks. We're talking less than two hundred dollars for both ceremony and reception, as opposed to the thousands some shell out for an occasion that stands a fifty-fifty chance of ending in divorce these days.

Most of Brother Joe's clients are in their thirties or older, and for many this isn't their first marriage. They have neither the desire nor the funds for a fancy shindig, they just want to be bound together in holy matrimony. Brother Joe offers them a little advice during the ceremony, where he admonishes them to be true, caring, kind and loving at all times.

Occasionally he gets a young couple that has "gotten themselves into trouble," i.e. the bride is knocked up. "Them don't last long generally," Joe relates. "Once the baby gits born they split up. Least this way the kid's got a name; he ain't no bastard."

Brother Joe has been a marriage minister for five years, ever since he was released from prison for selling moonshine. "Spent five years in the lockup on that one" he tells me. "Hitching people don't make as much money, but at least I ain't gotta worry about the damn still blowing up." Amen, Brother Joe.

## Art/dance/music instructor

There are people all over this land who are talented painters, dancers or musicians, and even more who wish they were. If you are musically or artistically gifted you can make money teaching others. This is a gig that can work even in small towns and rural areas. All you need is a studio (your home will usually do) and some students.

It's likely many of your clients will be kids, as parents always have visions of their children being the next Beethoven or Monet. A fair number of adults may seek you as well. The desire to create runs deep in the human soul.

Teaching can be a trying profession. For example, there are millions of people out there who can't carry a tune in a bucket yet think they're destined to be the next "American Idol." You'll need to exercise patience and tact in dealing with your customers. Whatever their real level of talent is, their hopes and dreams are precious to them. Treat them accordingly. Being the "delicate genius" may boost your ego but it'll destroy your client base.

# Chapter Five
## Case Histories

You'll, of course, need some basic equipment and supplies. If you're going to teach piano out of your home you will of course need a piano. If you teach guitar or violin you will have one of your own even though the student will bring theirs. A large, open room is necessary for dance instruction, and art teachers may want to keep supplies on hand for forgetful pupils.

I've seen people who do this put formal signs outside their home, listing their specialty and phone number. I used to live near a master piano player who advertised this way. She stayed very busy.

You can spread the word by doing free workshops at the local library or community center. Do an introductory lesson for free then invite those desiring more instruction to contact you. I would advise against using a web page if you're doing this for tax-free income. As always, take only cash or, if you must, a personal check made out to you.

This sort of business can actually do better in rural areas than the cities. Artists and musicians flock to metropolitan areas but often avoid the sticks. You may be the only person for a hundred miles with your specialty. Spread the word discreetly, give your students lots of attention and encouragement and you should do well.

### Beverly's Piano Lessons

Beverly Taylor lives in a small town about an hour from Atlanta, Georgia. Her husband is an engineer and commutes to the city every day. She is a piano teacher by trade but the local schools don't offer musical instruction. She has been doing the housewife thing for two years and is bored out of her skull.

Then one day she reads a book on the underground economy and is inspired. She creates an ad on her computer and prints it out. It tells a little about her and invites people interested in learning piano to call her. She puts the flyers up at the post office and also the bulletin board at her church.

She starts doing this in February and at first receives little response. But as the warm months approach she gets calls and emails from parents interested in having her teach their kids over the summer. She starts with three pupils that visit her once a week, ranging in age from nine to fourteen. She has her home piano professionally tuned and buys some instruction books, which she sells to her students at a modest profit. By summer's end she has a dozen kids and one adult taking lessons from her. The enterprise involves less than twenty hours a week of her time. She charges a modest fee of fifteen dollars per lesson, which brings her almost two hundred tax-free dollars a week.

She puts this money aside and eventually buys a second piano. The next summer she teaches beginners on one and advanced students on the other in a separate room. She is so busy she has two and sometimes three pupils at her house at the same time. Soon she raises her fee to twenty dollars a lesson and instructs year round. She is no longer bored. She enjoys teaching something she loves and the money helps her fix up the home. Her once dull routine has become an exciting and profitable sideline, thanks to the underground economy!

### Paid Companion

We're getting older, folks. There are over forty million people in the United States sixty-five and over. As the population ages the need for health care providers of all kinds will increase. Even if you have no medical skills whatsoever you can cash in by being a companion/provider.

Many of the aged still live in their own homes but require help with various tasks. Younger people may need similar care due to illness, injury or handicap. This is where you come in. Depending on the person's abilities you may do their shop-

## Chapter Five
## Case Histories

ping, cooking, or even bathe them and clean them up after a bowel movement. You may spend several hours a day with them or even live in the home. You will probably get a day off during the week, during which a friend or relative will fill in for you. Needless to say this kind of work requires compassion and patience.

You will likely deal with the person's family, and they will probably check you out nine ways from Sunday. You will probably need to endure a criminal records and even a drug check. The relatives may stick a surveillance camera in the home to make sure you're not abusing their loved one. Unfortunately there are some rotten apples that have beaten and even robbed the people they're caring for, and this has given the whole profession a tarnished image.

The money usually isn't that great, but you can save big if you live free with the person. This may or may not put a cramp on your lifestyle, depending on how you spend your spare time. Personally the most exciting thing I do these days is read books so I'd be ideal.

People who need to be cared for in this fashion can be difficult. They're often bitter about losing their independence and will take out their frustrations on you. Sometimes they suffer from Alzheimer's, muscular dystrophy, or other horrible ailments. They will have special needs you will have to tend to.

Death comes to all of us, and if you stay with the same person long enough they may very well kick off on your watch. There's nothing to do then but call the hospital and the family and wait for the ambulance to show up. You will probably be expected to attend the funeral. Oftentimes the family will give you a lump sum afterwards as a sort of bonus.

Depending on your temperament and personal strengths a gig like this can be sheer hell or a rewarding experience. Weigh it carefully before jumping in. It can be a tremendous opportunity for the right person.

## Mary and Flora

Mary was a young lady I went to college with. During her last two years of school she lived with an elderly woman near campus named Flora. She was in her early eighties and could walk and bathe herself, but needed someone to do her shopping and cooking.

Mary got to Flora's house about three o'clock every day. She checked on her to make sure she was okay, then went to the market, if necessary. She cooked dinner and served it about six PM; the two ate together. Mary also made sure that Flora took her medications and would often watch TV with her. About nine o'clock Flora would go to bed. Her home was large, and after retiring for the evening she left Mary free to do homework, relax, and even have friends over.

Flora slowly declined over time and Mary did more for her as she did, eventually bathing her and assisting her with other sanitary needs. Flora passed on quietly in her sleep late one evening and Mary discovered her. She called Flora's son, who handled things from that point on. A few months later Flora's kids sold her home.

Mary was happily surprised one afternoon when she received a call from the local Ford dealership. Flora's son had used some of the profits from the sale of the home to purchase a small economy car for her, in appreciation of the good care she gave his mother in the last years of her life.

## Bum

Okay, now we're getting to the fun part of the book. We're going to look at ways of making money that by their very nature belong wholly underground. Some sit on the edge of illegality, while others are weird, unethical or sleazy.

# Chapter Five
## Case Histories

The first of these is bum/beggar/panhandler. Unless you've spent your life confined to a cell you've run into these people before. They may just sit on the street corner with an empty cup and a sign that says "DONATIONS ACCEPTED – HOMELESS VET." Or maybe you've seen them standing on the entrance ramp to the highway with a sign that says WILL WORK FOR FOOD.

Another way they get you is to walk up to you in a parking lot or on the street. They hit you with a sob story about the kids being hungry or being out of town and having their wallet stolen. "I just need five bucks for gas, man!" they say. Then when you fork it over they repeat the same line to the next sucker.

First off, I don't recommend making your living this way; it's sleazy and bereft of any dignity. On the other hand, it helps to know how it's done, because you never know but that you might very well end up on the street, penniless and with no other way of making cash. In a situation like that knowing the ABCs of panhandling might keep you from starving or freezing to death.

The following advice comes from street people who were willing to talk to me, as well as a wonderful, but out of print little tome called *The Beggar's Handbook*, by none other than M.T. Pockets. You can still get copies of it from Amazon.com's network of used booksellers. Also try Abebooks.com, which sells only used and out of print books.

## Panhandling 101

1. Be clean and courteous — a filthy disheveled bum mumbling something about Roswell, New Mexico, and demanding spare change is going to jail before he makes his first buck. On the other hand, a line like "Pardon me, sir/ma'am, but I am down on my luck and haven't eaten in two days. Could you please spare a dollar or two?" spoken by some-

## Under the Table and Into Your Pocket
### The How and Why of the Underground Economy

one who is washed and wearing worn but clean clothes is a far more successful approach.

2. Forget the street corners — people associate them with hookers, drug peddlers, and other unwholesome ilk. Position yourself against an outside wall in the middle area of the block where pedestrians will walk past you. Then toss your pitch out.
3. Have a prop — a good example is a cup of pencils with a hand written note on it that says "FOR SALE — PLEASE PAY WHAT YOU CAN." This makes the mark think "Oh jeez, the scumbag is at least trying to sell something instead of just sticking his hand out." Chances are they'll give you a dollar or two without daring to touch your "merchandise."

   Another approach is to have a photo of you in a military uniform, standing in front of the flag, sitting beside you in a cheap gold frame. Alongside it have a note that says "I WAS INJURED WHILE DEFENDING YOU. NOW NOBODY CARES. PLEASE HELP."

   Have a story to go along with this, like how your back was shattered when you jumped on a mine to save your buddies during the Gulf War. Tell them how after they removed half the discs in your back they cut off your pension and now it hurts every time you take a breath. You'll either collect a fortune or get the shit beat out of you by a real vet who can see through your lies. Come to think of it, I'd beat the shit out of you myself.
4. Reward the Giver — very few people are totally selfless. Even the kind-hearted among us expect something in return for their compassion, usually an affirmation that they really are good people. So toss them a "Thank you, sir! And God bless you for your kindness!" Try to be sincere.

# Chapter Five
# Case Histories

## Profile

Ed B. is a professional beggar in downtown Athens, Georgia. He is actually a part-time student at the nearby University of Georgia, where he is majoring in sociology. He started panhandling as part of a class project on homelessness, but found the money was so good he never stopped.

Ed dresses the part in his apartment. He puts on faded jeans with holes at the knees, an old tee shirt he picked up at Goodwill, and a pair of off brand sneakers he got at Wal-Mart a couple of years back. An old ball cap completes the ensemble. In winter he wears an Army jacket he picked up in a surplus store. "It keeps me warm but still conveys a sense of poverty," he relates.

Ed positions himself on a block that is dominated by "alternative"-type businesses. There is a head shop, a Goth clothing store, a vegetarian restaurant, and a club named the Insane Cockatiel. He is tolerated by the guilt-ridden liberals and naïve idealists that frequent these places.

Once he tried hanging out a few blocks away, in front of a furniture store where "regular" people shop. Tips were good for the half hour he was there. Then the cops ran him off. Now he sticks with the areas that students go to.

The University of Georgia has almost 30,000 students, so he has never been recognized by any of his classmates. Ed uses a prop: a large tin filled with crap he picked up at a flea market: erasers, tie clips, old batteries, little laminated cards with Jesus stuff written on them, some ancient CDs, etc. It sits on the sidewalk next to a larger tin where people drop money. "Please look at my stuff," he says to those who pass by. "I'm just trying to make enough to eat."

On average this gig brings him anywhere from $25-$50 for four or five hours of "work." He gets more at Christmas, sometimes as much as a hundred bucks. "The season brings

# Under the Table and Into Your Pocket
The How and Why of the Underground Economy

out the best in humanity," he tells me, as he chomps down on the burger I bought him. He usually only begs on weekends.

Ed is a trust fund brat, so the money he makes is pure spending cash. "It covers my cigs, my drinking habit, and the daily paper," he says. He offers one bit of advice: "If someone on the street hits you up for money, look at their teeth. If they're not gnarled as hell then they're con artists." Then he flashes me a smile with his pearly white chompers.

## Selling Your Body

We're not talking hookers here. We'll be looking at three different ways to sell yourself: by being a human guinea pig, by peddling products like plasma and sperm, and by working as a professional tease. A tease is someone who gets some poor sucker aroused then lets him take care of it on his own.

When the subject turns to selling body parts, images pop up of shady hotel rooms, and drugged men lying in bathtubs filled with ice, the victims of professional kidney thieves. Forget that nonsense. If there is a way to actually sell kidneys, corneas, limbs, etc., then I haven't found it. When I tried to track down sources I got nowhere.

That being said, let's look at being a guinea pig. In the U.S. it takes years, sometimes up to a decade, to get a new drug approved. Part of the process involves tests on human subjects.

This is where you come in. You can find out about these gigs through ads on the radio or the papers (the alternative press seems rife with ads from testing firms). Basically you volunteer to take a new drug and let the doctors monitor how it affects you. In exchange you get free meds, a checkup, and eventually some cash.

In order to qualify you must have a condition the new medicine can treat. For example, if it's a pill to reduce cholesterol they're going to want you to have a lot of it already in your ar-

# Chapter Five
## Case Histories

teries. If it's a drug to make you lose weight they're going to want some lard asses to try it out.

The treatment period can last from a few weeks to months on end. Though sometimes you are confined to a dormitory with other guinea pigs, in most instances you'll be allowed to go about your daily life. They will want you in every week or two to look you over. You'll probably be required to record your reactions to the stuff they're squirting in you.

Forget using this gig as a basis for a lawsuit. You'll be signing iron-clad release agreements agreeing to hold the clinic harmless if your brain explodes or your blood turns to syrup and you keel over dead. The drug corporations know all about CYA.

This gig can get you a few hundred bucks, but most of them don't pay till the end of the experiment. Their benefit lies more in the free medical treatment you get. For example, a diabetic without health insurance can get his testing supplies free, as well as drugs to treat his condition. See the profile at the end of the chapter, where I describe my experiences as a guinea pig.

### *Gimme hair, long, beautiful hair!*

I love being bald. I no longer worry about changing styles, fighting dandruff, or finding the right barber. But I'm the exception. Most people will do anything to avoid losing their precious locks. The anti-baldness industry is a multi-billion dollar part of our economy.

One of the common solutions to this "problem" is a process known as weaving, where another person's strands are sewn onto a folically-challenged person's scalp. If your own hair is long and lustrous you can make big bucks by peddling it for this purpose. Go to websites like www.hairworks.com for the lowdown. Wig makers are another market.

## Under the Table and Into Your Pocket
The How and Why of the Underground Economy

### *Professional Masturbators*

Is it your dream to get paid for spanking the monkey? If you're young, smart, and healthy it can come true. Frozen sperm is a $164,000,000 a year industry. It's fueled by the growing number of women who want a kid, but don't want or can't find a husband. Lesbian couples are a growing segment of the customer base as well.

This details sound too good to be true. You're led into a room with comfortable furniture, a TV playing X-rated videos, and a big stack of porno mags. They leave you alone with a cup while you let your mind run wild. In return for your life juices you can get as much as $100, plus a $1,000 bonus every six months just for sticking with the program. College kids can "earn" as much as $6,000 an academic year, a low enough amount that the IRS is highly unlikely to bug you, but still plenty of cash for beer and pizza. Ah, to be 18 again!

The catch to this gig is that the clinics are very picky. They look for handsome young men with athletic ability, good health, and high IQs. For example, California Cryobank, a leading firm (heh, heh — I wrote "firm!") in the business rejects 95% of their applicants. The average order is for a guy who is over six feet tall with blonde hair and blue eyes who is majoring in the sciences.

You must also be comfortable with the idea that you've sired hundreds of children you'll never see. The average "donation" can produce ten kids. If you can pass the test and handle the stress, though, the world can be yours!

### *The Wonderful World of Plasma Donation*

On the other hand, if you're fat, stupid, and ugly then you can still make a few bucks peddling your internal liquids. In

## Chapter Five
## Case Histories

your case the desired commodity is your blood, or more specifically the platelets in your blood that form plasma. The money's not as good as the sperm donors get, but there is a cup of grapefruit juice and some cookies waiting for you at the end of the ordeal.

There are 400 centers around the country that accept plasma from some 400,000 donors. In order to donate one must be between 18 and 59 and HIV free (they'll ask you embarrassing questions about whether you've been with hookers or shot up dope). Some clinics require you to have a verifiable street address as well, and others won't let anyone who's gotten a tattoo in the last year participate.

As mentioned before you're not actually donating blood. The clinic is harvesting the platelets in your blood, which are used to make medicines for hemophiliacs and other wonderful things. They'll insert a huge needle deep into your veins. A hose on the end sends your blood flowing into a centrifuge that spins the liquid around to separate out the platelets. It then sends it back into your body. First time donors often faint.

Most clinics will pay around $45 for two visits a week. You get like $15 the first time, then $30 when you return a few days later. You get the money on the spot.

I visited the plasma clinic in Spartanburg, South Carolina, one time. The donors were mostly street people and other desperate individuals. The building was dirty and old, and the whole atmosphere was depressing.

There is one bright spot in all this bleakness: there are people with certain rare blood types who are in high demand by the clinics. These people have to suffer through the same procedure, but they can make as much as $200 a week doing this.

If you know your blood type then you may want to call your local clinic; look in the Yellow Pages under "blood" or "plasma." Or just ask a bum. You might be one your way to a high paying gig.

## Profile

Your jolly author is a diabetic, and I found myself at one point in my life with no insurance and little money. My blood sugars were running almost three times higher than normal. I was perpetually tired, my joints ached, and I pissed all the time.

Did I bitch and moan and demand government help? No! I found a newspaper ad placed by a local clinic. They were testing a new form of insulin and needed diabetics to be guinea pigs.

I went down and signed up. In return they loaded me up on medication, as well as a blood monitor, test strips and everything else needed to control my condition. They even tossed in a tee shirt (size small — it comes down to my nipples) and a free clock.

The insulin was a new synthetic form that hit the blood stream immediately. I had to inject it twice a day, and also check my blood sugars every twelve hours. I kept a log of the readings and turned it in every two weeks when I went back to the clinic.

The folks there were very nice and helped me out in a lot of ways. For example, about two months into the test my allergies kicked up. They gave me tons of free Claritin. They also gave me nutritional counseling, which is why I'm munching on diet potato chips as I write these words.

The trial was scheduled to run nine months, but I got a job about halfway through that offered health insurance so I dropped out. Had I stuck with it I would have gotten a check for three hundred bucks, but I couldn't keep my new job and also make my bi-weekly trips to the clinic. Oh well. You know, these fat free sour cream and onion chips really suck. Run out and get me a chocolate shake, willya?

## Chapter Five
## Case Histories

### Other Under the Radar Ways to Make Money

There are literally thousands of ways to make tax-free income and in this book I've tried to touch on as many as I could. There are plenty of other ideas I have learned about and I want to share them briefly in this section.

I have a friend who went on a hunting trip to Wyoming one time. Now if you've ever been to that state you know it's basically one huge wasteland except around the mountains. He asked a couple of locals how they survived economically. "I hunt for jade," one of them said. The other replied, "I shoot coyotes."

Jade is a semi-precious substance used in jewelry and found in mineral deposits. If you are a rock hound and locate it, you can sell it to jewelry makers for a good price. Other people look for fossils, pick wild mushrooms, and scour the woods for ginseng. All of these can be found for free and sold for a tidy profit.

As far as shooting coyotes, the government no longer pays you to kill them. But various state and county agencies offer bounties from time to time on animals that prey on livestock or are a danger to agriculture in general. Check without your local wildlife authority in your area. A related opportunity is trapping beavers and other animals for their pelts; a game warden can tell you more about this.

Earlier we talked about making money as a minister. A similar opportunity exists for Tarot Card experts, palm readers, séance holders, and others versed in New Age/Occult practices. Some say these are legitimate services, others call them scams. I call them neither, I'm just letting you know they exist and I have been told they can be quite profitable.

I knew a bill collector one time that was between jobs. He made ends meet by doing freelance work for local video rental

# Under the Table and Into Your Pocket
## The How and Why of the Underground Economy

stores. He obtained lists of people who had kept rented tapes for extended periods of time and went to their homes asking for them. He got five bucks for each tape he recovered and half of whatever late fees he collected at the door.

Wooden pallets can be had for free near dumpsters and construction sites. They can be chopped into firewood and sold by the bundle or truckload. Rotting brush and trees can be turned into mulch and sold to gardeners and landscapers.

Ever watch the *Beverly Hillbillies* TV show? If so you may remember that Jethro was fond of "crawdads." Actually these are small crayfish that looks like little lobsters. Lots of people love to eat them. You can find them in streams or raise them yourself in a tank.

If you have a green thumb you can raise flowers and/or vegetables and sell them on street corners, on the roadside or at local flea or farmer's markets. Learn basic floral design from a book or a community college class to create nice arrangements that will earn you a good income. You can also buy plants from a floral or produce warehouse instead of growing your own.

Isolated businesses are frequently targeted for burglary because the police rarely patrol the area where they're located. You can make money running a private patrol/security service, cruising by these places three or four times a night, shining a spotlight on them and making sure the doors are locked.

Pet sitting is a growing business. People go on vacation and don't want to stick their animals in kennels. So they leave them in the house and hire you to check on them every day or two. You make sure they are okay, give them fresh food and water, and sometimes clean up poop.

Car salesman will usually pay someone to "bird dog" for them. You find someone who wants to buy an automobile and steer them towards your associate at the dealership, who hands you two or three hundred bucks for each sale you send his

## Chapter Five
## Case Histories

way. Insurance, real estate and other peddlers often do the same thing.

Writers who still use typewriters or pen their words longhand often hire someone to enter their manuscripts into a computer. Magazines like *Writer's Digest* carry ads from people who do this.

In an earlier section we talked about selling blood, sperm, plasma and other bodily products for cash. In India and other nations you can legally sell a kidney for up to fifty thousand dollars. Don't try this in the U.S. though.

And the opportunities go on and on. People need garages cleaned out, errands ran, wood chopped, brush cleared, feet rubbed, broken windows replaced, hair cut, etc., etc. *ad infinitum*. Remember Thomas Edison's formula for success: "find a need and fill it." Do so and you'll always be able to make a cash income. It's all up to you, your ambition and willingness to work. So use your mind and muscles and if nothing else you'll never starve. Good luck!

# Chapter Six
# Red Light Work

## Strippers

They're called "exotic dancers" these days, but that's a BS term made up by lawyers who defend club owners. Not much skill involved here. You dance for an audience that crams cash into your underwear and your orifices as you undress one piece at a time. Most of the gigs are for younger women, but guys who are cute and buff can get in as well.

The tax-free aspect of this comes in where salary is concerned. There isn't one. In fact, strippers usually have to pay a nightly or weekly fee to the club to let them dance. As I said before they get their money from cash tips, which can be quite generous. It's not unusual at all for a hot dancer to walk away with five or six hundred bucks a night, mostly in ones and fives.

Usually they dance on a stage, often clinging to a metal pole that they swing around in the nude. Strippers make extra bucks by doing table dances or lap dances, for which they get a minimum amount. Table dancing is just that: they dance on a guy's table while he sucks back drinks and wishes he could touch his cock.

A lap dance consists of writhing around on a guy's lap. He can't touch, though. He has to keep his hands apart and away from the girl. Remember what I said about this gig being one giant tease?

Another way to make extra bucks is off of men who fall in love with dancers. There are tons of guys out there whose

# Under the Table and Into Your Pocket
## The How and Why of the Underground Economy

ultimate fantasy is to date a stripper, and there are many more that are lonely as hell and go to the clubs desperate to find companionship. A smart girl can milk these losers for drinks, jewelry, clothes, even cars.

It used to be "in" for women to go see male strippers, but this isn't nearly as big as it once was. Guys who want to break into this gig may have to dance for gay men. That may or may not be an appealing thought. In cities like New Orleans and San Francisco passable cross dressers and shemales dance for big crowds. Lesbians can find spots dancing for other women in many larger cities.

The successful female stripper will have giant boobs, nice lips and lots of hair. Many of them get plastic surgery to raise the equipment up to standard. Guys will need six pack abs and a big cock. A full head of hair isn't necessary but it does help.

Stripping may sound like a fun way to make big bucks, but I can't recommend it. That's because I have seen too many girls get screwed. The lifestyle gets 'em almost every time. They're flattered by all the attention guys give them and start partying all the time. As their looks fade they're forced to work skankier and skankier dives, until they finally bottom out and become street walkers.

I used to live in a town that had three big strip clubs. I knew girls who started out at the nice one near the airport, a joint called the Trophy Club, where the dancers were all babes and the clients had loads of cash. After a few months they would lose their spot to fresher and unspoiled faces. They then had to go to Godiva's, where working class guys hung out. Their tips shrank along with the choice of quality men. Finally they worked their way down to a rat trap on the poor side of town called Ladies and Lace. By this time they were usually doubling as prostitutes.

## Chapter Six
### Red Light Work

**Dominatrix**

Would you pay someone to tie you up, gag you, call you every foul name in the book and beat you with a whip? Plenty of people do. That leads us into our final underground career option.

Both men and women make money dominating other people, but most of the pros are females. They cater to men who find pleasure in pain, torture, humiliation, and denial. This gig is even more profitable than stripping, with the added benefit that you don't have to be nice to your clients. In fact, most of them prefer the dominant to be a cold, mean-spirited bitch.

A lot of ladies pick up clients by cruising adult chat rooms, especially the ones on AOL. They start talking to some poor schmuck, get him wound up, then tell him he can have the real thing for two hundred bucks an hour. Some dominatrixes limit themselves to men in their geographical area. Others will go nationwide, provided their client pays for transportation on top of her fees.

The sweet part about this deal is that it preys on the customer's sexual appetites, but since sex isn't normally involved it dodges anti-prostitution laws. A typical session may involve meeting a guy at a hotel room, cuffing or tying him down, beating him with a whip, and maybe burning his nipples with hot candle wax or urinating on him.

When it's all over the woman unties the dude, collects her cash and goes. If he wants to masturbate after she leaves she'll hit him up for an extra fifty for her "permission." A good dominatrix can make several hundred dollars in one night off of two or three one-hour sessions like this.

Some women do this strictly for the money, but others genuinely enjoy the feeling of power it gives them. A lot of these go a little further than most of their colleagues. They start offering "feminization" services, where they'll make the guy shave off all his body hair then put women's undies on him. The hard core ones will also do him up in makeup and put him in a wig and mini-skirt. The client pays for all this stuff of course.

Dominatrixes often run their own "dungeon." This can be the basement of their home or a room at a club which they stock with torture devices. Select clients pay big fees to experience such joys as being hung from the ceiling and whipped.

Some are "forced" to have sex with other guys. A small number of dominatrixes assist their clients in getting on female hormones, obtaining breast implants, and even finding a doctor who'll chop off their cock and remove their testicles.

Once they do this the dominatrix may even let the castrated, emasculated half-man live with them as a full time slave. He/it loses all rights, including the right to experience pleasure of any kind.

This gig is perfect for the underground economy as payment is always in cash. Plus it is very, very unlikely that any clients will ever squeal to the IRS. After all, what guy wants it publicly known that he once paid a thousand bucks to be dressed up like Dolly Parton and kicked in the groin?

## *Profile*

Victoria is a professional "domme" (short for dominatrix) that I met in an AOL chat room while doing official and dispassionate academic research solely for this book. During our rather interesting conversation she informed me that she had been working in the field for 10 years. She explained that she had been a controlling person all her life, and distrusted strong willed men. She also expressed a belief that women were innately superior to males, who she described as "under evolved."

## Chapter Six
## Red Light Work

Victoria is a specialist in "feminization," making a man more feminine in appearance and thought. She employs a variety of techniques, including hypnosis, sensory deprivation, sensory overload, and pleasure reinforcement. She leads men to doubt their "manliness" and embrace lady-like behavior.

Victoria sent me a picture of herself via email. She is attractive, with ample breasts and the look of a "strict librarian" about her. I guessed her age to be late 30s – early 40s.

Things took a strange turn when Victoria asked me if I wanted to go to a "bondage convention" in Las Vegas with her. I told her that it sounded like fun, but I had a model train convention in Chicago that weekend to go to, and I couldn't stand to miss the excitement. She called me many unpleasant things.

Towards the end of the talk she sent me more pictures of herself, including a nude one. I couldn't help but notice that, between her long legs and beneath her huge bosom, there was a large, very stiff penis. That's right," "she" said when I asked her about it. "I'm a girl with something extra to offer." At that point unforeseen problems caused my computer to fail. Soon after I switched my ISPs and have never looked back.

### Summing Up

Well, it's been a wild ride, from the signing of the Declaration of Independence to a chat with a castrating shemale. Along the way we have discussed history, philosophy, politics, economics and psychology. We've learned some very disturbing facts about our government and the IRS. And we've made the company of some heroic people who have taken responsibility for their lives away from Big Brother.

The underground economy is and will continue to be a vital part of American economic life. The government may try to curb its growth but it can never do so for long. For it is the purest and most natural expression of human freedom, the freedom to invent, to trade, to mutually benefit from others. Its light may dim from time to time but it can never be extinguished,

I appreciate you taking this journey with me. And wherever your own goals and efforts lead you I wish you all the best. Keep your minds open, your paths straight and your eyes focused ahead. Excelsior!

Bill Wilson<br/>
February 2005

# Appendix

## How to Make Money from Storage Building Auctions

Buying and selling is a time-honored way of making a living. However, like any profession, success in merchandising requires following some fundamental rules. The most basic of these is to obtain items of good quality that people will actually want to purchase, and to acquire them at a low enough cost to ensure adequate profit. Once this challenge is met, the entrepreneur's success is largely assured.

Fortunately, across the United States a huge supply of desirable products exists for low prices. Furniture, electronics, appliances, clothing, books, art, toys, tools and a plethora of other goodies can be had for a fraction of their true value. The purchasers can use these items themselves, or resell them for a generous markup. Startup costs are minimal; a van or pickup truck (a trailer towed by a car will do) and a few hundred dollars are all that is required to begin your own business.

I am not talking about raiding dumpsters, joining wholesale clubs, or fencing stolen merchandise. I am discussing public storage buildings, which you can find in virtually any community coast to coast. Millions of individuals and businesses use these facilities to store all sorts of goods. Many of them eventually fall behind on their monthly rental bills. After an extended period of non-payment the storage building owner can legally claim the items. He or she will often hold periodic public auctions to sell off the goods, in order to recoup a portion of their lost rent.

It is important to remember that the USA has become a nation of pack rats. Consumers acquire all sorts of things that they will never need or even use. Impulse purchases, seasonal items, unwanted gifts — all these and more end up under lock

## Under the Table and Into Your Pocket
The How and Why of the Underground Economy

and key for extended periods. Seniors selling a large home and moving to a smaller one realize they have tons of unwanted possessions. Singles or couples buy a new sofa, DVD player or television and store the old one. Children grow up and leave home, and the parents hold on to their clothing, old musical instruments, books and clothing for sentimental reasons. Businesses upgrade their computer systems frequently, and the original PCs are seen as obsolete; they are put "on ice." Ours is truly a throw-away society.

The result of all this financial fickleness is that large quantities of perfectly good things end up in rented storage buildings. Then death, financial hardship, or just plain apathy or forgetfulness kick in, and the items are forgotten. This is where the real opportunities for *you* come in. The units range in size from twenty-five square feet up to several hundred. Some are even climate-controlled, and may contain freezers full of fresh meat or other perishable goods. Chances are, there is such a place near you right now, packed with all sorts of treasures, waiting for you to claim them!

The first step in taking advantage of this opportunity is learning when the auctions in your area take place. Get a copy of the local Yellow Pages directory and look under "storage facilities." Contact the offices. Make sure you do not call storage building dealers, the people who sell the little sheds you see in back yards nationwide. You want the businesses that rent their own units on their own property.

Ask for the owner or manager, and tell them you want to know when the next auction is going to be. Some places hold them on a regular basis, and can give you the exact date and time. Others hold them "as need arises," but do not currently have one planned. Put these on a call back list, and check with them once a month or so. Still others put a notice in the newspaper when the time for the auction approaches. Learn what paper they use and watch its classifieds.

## *Appendix*

On the day of the auction, show up a few minutes before it begins, ready to do some heavy lifting. A pickup or other large truck is ideal. A van is great, but there might be some head room problems. A bigger car can work if you use a utility trailer as well. You will also need work gloves, tarps or blankets to cover the items in case of rain, and, if possible, hand trucks and/or a partner. Of course, you will also need a place to store your purchases for a while until you sell them.

Bidding at auctions is an art form unto itself. You may wish to just watch others at the first two or three you attend, just to get a feel for how much items go for. Keep in mind that your primary goal is resale. Don't bid three hundred dollars on a building full of goods that you can only make fifty bucks on. A good idea is to check local flea markets, yard sales, classifieds, salvage stores, eBay, etc., to see what different items go for.

The auctioneer will open the buildings one at a time to let the bidders see what they contain. If most or all of the goods are in boxes, then he or she will break these open and display their contents to the crowd. Bring a pad and pen, and try to estimate the approximate resale value of the merchandise. Then place your highest bid at no more than fifty percent of that amount. If in doubt about the profitability of the contents, then don't bid; there is always another day, and you don't want to get stuck with tons of unwanted junk filling up *your* storage area.

As discussed before, the variety of things you can find at these auctions is astounding. Appliances, furniture, electronics, books, clothes, toys, pet supplies, CDs, records and cassettes, VHS/DVD movies, and boxes filled with knick-knacks are common finds. Cash, jewelry, gold and silver coins, even automobiles have been found. You want to look the stuff over as thoroughly as possible, to make sure that rain has not leaked in and destroyed things. If you smell mildew or see

## Under the Table and Into Your Pocket
The How and Why of the Underground Economy

evidence of water damage, then pass that building up. Mice and other rodents sometimes get in, but they rarely do much damage, except to clothing and stored food (speaking of clothing, check the pockets and linings of any you get. Old people hide money in them. Wads of cash have been found stuffed in shoes and mattresses). Storage buildings with shingle roofs and heavy, tight-fitting doors do the best job of preserving stored items.

Okay, the auction is over, and you were the high bidder on one or more lots. You can usually claim your merchandise on the spot. Start going through your acquisitions immediately. You want to separate the good stuff from the absolute junk, which you will haul to the dump. One strategy is to break open the boxes and hold up nice finds while other bidders are still milling about. Quite often they will make purchases from you right there!

Sometimes you will obtain things that need a little work. This is where a working knowledge of electronics, appliance repair and/or woodworking comes in handy. You may locate a color television that only needs an inexpensive part to get it working again. Lawn mowers, garden tillers and the like are often cast aside as "broke," when all they need is a spark plug or other minor repair. A clothes dryer may only require a new lint filter to run like new. Scuffed or dirty furniture can be cleaned and polished. Learn to see past the dust and dents to discern an item's true value. Many people have furnished their own homes this way, and saved hundreds if not thousands of dollars doing so.

Store your stuff carefully. Stack it neatly, cover it with tarps or blankets, make sure the weather will not get in, and lay out some poison in case vermin get in. Write down your inventory, noting general condition and what you think you can get for each item.

*Appendix*

111

Now you can look at selling your goods. The venues for doing this are numerous. Newspaper ads are a good bet for larger or pricier items. People scan the classifieds every day looking for bargains. In addition, many local radio stations have weekly "swap shops," usually on weekend mornings, where you can call in, tell what you have for sale, and leave your phone number for interested parties. Call nearby broadcasters to find out about these. Sometimes television stations offer the same service.

Flea markets, also called "swap meets," are great places to sell things. Check your local area for them. *The Official Guide To U.S. Flea Markets*, by Kitty Werner, is a nationwide listing of markets. The office will rent you one or more tables to display your merchandise on; fees range from three or four dollars a day per table up to fifteen or twenty for one inside a building with climate control. Check with the manager for prices and procedures for dealers. At some markets you can just show up the day of the sale and claim your own space; others require you to pay a few days in advance. Visit the market on a sale day before you bring your goods out; make sure there is good customer flow.

Be sure and bring plenty of change, bags for the purchases (available at any grocery store; just offer them a few bucks for forty or fifty of their sacks), a comfortable chair to sit in, and a cooler with drinks and some food. A beach umbrella can keep you cool in warm months. Bring a book or portable radio to help the time pass. Covering your tables with tarps, blankets or heavy paper makes your display more appealing to the eye. Wide varieties of rather colorful folks both sell and buy at the markets, and you should meet some interesting people. For more information, check out *How To Make Cash Money Selling At Swap Meets, Flea Markets, Etc.,* by Jordan Cooper, available from Loompanics.

# Under the Table and Into Your Pocket
The How and Why of the Underground Economy

Yard or garage sales are another way to rake in the dough. If you have a home with a good-sized yard or a carport or garage, this option can work for you. Make sure you have plenty of change for your customers, as well as bags for their purchases. Advertise the upcoming sale in your local paper, put up signs in the neighborhood stating the day and address of the sale, and be outside early, ready to do business — yard sale fans are early risers! The old pros at this business set their merchandise out the night before, and cover it with tarps, so they do not have to set up the morning of the sale.

In many rural areas and small towns, retail auctions are a favorite form of entertainment. Dealers bring truckloads of products they have bought wholesale elsewhere and put them up for bid one at a time. Forget any images you may have of rich people wearing fancy clothing and buying rare antiques or Kennedy memorabilia. These sales are frequented by working class and country folk, the same types you will see at the flea market.

You can make a hefty profit by selling at these auctions, but you need to know what you are doing. Find out when and where they are held by checking your Yellow Pages, local papers, or just asking around. Go several times before you decide to sell. Watch the bidders and the auctioneer. Talk to the manager and find out what the terms are; usually the house will get a portion of whatever money you make. Retail auctions can be great fun as well as lucrative.

In many parts of the country it is legal to set up an impromptu storefront along the roadside, in front of abandoned stores or in the hinterlands of large parking lots. Cops will not hassle you as long as no one complains. In the South it is common to see people selling produce, clothing, decorator rugs, stuffed animals, or other goods right off the back of their trucks or out of a van. The northeastern states seem much less tolerant of this form of free enterprise, however. The rule of

*Appendix*

thumb is this: if you see others doing it without being persecuted, then you can do it to. Gas stations and convenience stores that have gone out of business are great locales. Bring your stuff and set it out for customers to see. Leave plenty of parking room, and expect many people to drive past your setup while checking out the goods.

Other venues include pawn shops, web pages, and collectors. It is amazing what people will collect. Campaign buttons, old books, walking sticks, teddy bears, shaving razors, beer mugs, and even prepaid calling cards have their enthusiasts. Read a few books on antiques and collectibles to become conversant on the subject. Internet sites like eBay are great as well.

No matter how great a sales person you are, you will eventually end up with some goods that just will not move. You can often sell these in bulk to other dealers at a low price. Charities like the Salvation Army and Goodwill will give you a receipt for donated items that you can use to reduce your taxes.

America is a fantastic place to live, with wealth literally overflowing its containers. It is quite possible to live off the fat of the land, even in these days. Storage building auctions offer fantastic opportunities for the entrepreneur. I should know; I have been benefiting from them for years. Now you can too. Good luck!

## Works Cited/Resources for Further Study

Aslett, Don. *Cleaning Up for a Living*. Cincinnati, Better Way Books, 1991.

Benson, Ragnar. *Survivalist's Medicine Chest*. Boulder, CO, Paladin Press. 1982.

Bruno, Leone, ed., *The War on Drugs: Opposing Viewpoints.* San Diego, CA, Greenhaven Press, 1998.

Churchill, Ward and Jim Vander Wall, *Agents of Oppression.* Cambridge MA, South End Press, 2002.

Evangelista, Anita. *How to Develop a Low-Cost Family Food-Storage System.* Port Townsend, WA, Breakout Productions, 1995.

Funicello, Theresa, *Tyranny of Kindness.* New York, Atlantic Monthly Press, 1993.

Gross, Martin, *The Education Racket.* New York, Bantam, 1995.

Gross, Martin, *The Government Racket.* New York, Bantam, 1992.

Gross, Martin, *The Tax Racket.* New York, Ballantine Books, 1995.

Hentoff, Nat, *The War on the Bill of Rights.* New York, Seven Stories Press, 2003.

Koenigsberg, David. *Handyman's Handbook.* New York, McGraw-Hill, 2003.

Lilly, Don. *How to Earn $15 to $50 an Hour and More With a Pickup Truck or Van.* Ballwin, MO, Darian Books, 1998.

Olasky, Marvin, *The Tragedy of American Compassion.* Washington, Regnery Publishing, 1992.

Piven, Frances Fax and Richard Cloward, *Regulating the Poor.* New York, Pantheon Books, 1971.

Rand, Ayn, *The Virtue of Selfishness.* New York, Signet, 1961.

Romney, Ed, *Living Well on Practically Nothing.* Boulder, CO, Paladin Press, 2001.

*Appendix*

Sands, Trent. *Personal Privacy Through Foreign Investing, Second Edition.* Port Townsend, WA, Breakout Productions, 2000.

Stanley, Thomas and William Danko, *The Millionaire Next Door.* New York, Pocket Books, 1996.

# YOU WILL ALSO WANT TO READ:

☐ **64266 DEEP INSIDE THE UNDERGROUND ECONOMY, How Millions of Americans are Practicing Free Enterprise in an Unfree Society,** *by Adam Cash.* Are you fed up with giving so much of your hard earned cash to the government then watching it get spent on ridiculous pork barrel special interest projects? Would you like to hold on to more of your money for your own special interest projects? The underground economy continues to grow in spite of the ever-widening attempts by the administration to regulate and tax everything we do. Millions of Americans are practicing free enterprise. You, too, can beat the system and operate your business tax-free as a "guerrilla capitalist." This is the book that will show you the ropes. *2003, 8½ x 11, 240 pp, soft cover.* **$24.95.**

☐ **13077 HOW TO MAKE CASH MONEY SELLING AT SWAP MEETS, FLEA MARKETS, ETC.,** *by Jordan Cooper.* You can make cash money selling at swap meets, flea markets, etc. as a part-time or full-time business. Several years ago, Jordan Cooper found himself laid off and without an income. He and his wife held a yard sale, and then took the leftover items to a local swap meet. In one day, they took in several hundred dollars. He hasn't worked a regular job since. His tips and how-to's were learned in the School of Hard Knocks, and can save you some hard knocks of your own. A low initial investment is all that is required, you can still hold your regular job while you're getting started, and you will be your own boss. *1988, 5½ x 8½, 177 pp, illustrated, soft cover.* **$12.95.**

☐ **64145 SHADOW MERCHANTS, Successful Retailing Without a Storefront,** *by Jordan Cooper.* In *Shadow Merchants,* Jordan Cooper continues your education in unconventional ways to make money without having a job or owning a conventional retail business. Included are a low initial investment; part-time or full-time; mobility; and much, much more. *1993, 5½ x 8½, 143 pp, illustrated, soft cover. $12.95.*

☐ **64167 SECOND-HAND SUCCESS, How to Turn Discards into Dollars, by *Jordan Cooper*.** *Second-Hand Success* is the story of successful merchants who turn discards into dollars. In the continuing education of earning a tax-free income, Jordan Cooper reveals the tricks used by dozens of clever entrepreneurs who turn trash into treasures. *1997, 5½ x 8½, 197 pp, illustrated, soft cover. $14.95.*

☐ **14099 THE ART & SCIENCE OF DUMPSTER DIVING, *by John Hoffman*.** This amazing manual tells you exactly how to dive dumpsters for fun and profit. Written by a life-long dumpster diver, the author shows you how to get just about anything you want or need — food, clothing, furniture, building materials, entertainment, luxury goods, tools, toys — you name it — ABSOLUTELY FREE. This manual guides you through the back alleys of America where amazing wealth is carelessly discarded. Hoffman will show you where to find the good stuff, how to rescue it and how to use it. All in all, it's a counterculture extravaganza, a practical course in urban survival, and a rollicking good read. *1993, 8½ x 11, 152 pp, illustrated, photographs, soft cover. $14.95.*

☐ **64210 THE TEMP WORKER'S GUIDE TO SELF-FULFILLMENT, How to slack off, achieve your dreams, and get paid for it!, *by Dennis Fiery*.** Temporary employment, or "temp work," can be a treasure trove of opportunity for the dedicated practitioner. Rather than being in a series of dead-end or meaningless short-term jobs, temp work offers numerous advantages. Author Dennis Fiery, who has temped in many industries, including ad agencies, book publishers, magazines, retail shops, fashion studios, financial companies, telecommunications and technology firms, educational institutions, and government offices, has learned how to effectively exploit and undermine the temp system. This invaluable book contains all the information needed to successfully obtain steady, good-paying work as a temp, while effectively satisfying the requirements of the employers who are seeking competent temp workers and fulfilling your own special needs. *1997, 5½ x 8½, 156 pp, illustrated, soft cover.* $12.95.

☐ **64240 MAKE $$$ AS A NON-FICTION WRITER,** *by Duncan Long.* You want to write, but how do you break into the field? Duncan Long, author and teacher, with over 30 years experience as a non-fiction writer, shows you the ropes. Find out: If you have the right "stuff" to become a writer; What are realistic expectations of income as a writer?; Do you have to use an agent?; Is freelancing your only option?; What kind of workspace and equipment do you need?; How to find those elusive writing assignments; How to pitch your own ideas; Methods of dealing with writer's block; What your finished work should look like when it's sent; How to present yourself professionally. If you've been wanting to make writing your full- or part-time career, don't put it off any longer! Let Duncan Long show you how to get started today. *2000, 5½ x 8½, 219 pp, soft cover.* $14.95.

☐ **64267 JOBS YOUR MOTHER NEVER WANTED YOU TO HAVE, An Alternative Career Guide,** *by Carolina Vegas Starr.* Looking for something a little bit off the beaten track for a career change? Bored with the job you have now and wonder if there is an obscure and unusual method of work you might be able to indulge yourself with and still make a living? How about a flamer, Irish-moss gatherer, wafer cleaner, arm-pit sniffer? If you answered yes to that question, this is the book for you. Not only will you find out about the above career choices, but a host of others, everything from Embalmer to a Zamboni driver. Dozens of jobs you never even knew existed, until now. These are jobs your mother may never have wanted you to have, but she isn't the one stuck in a mind numbing, boring, drone-clone job. This alternative career guide points out many different directions you can head towards finding your perfect job. *2003, 5½ x 8½, 152 pp, soft cover. $8.95.*

☐ **64129 SELL YOURSELF TO SCIENCE, The Complete Guide to Selling Your Organs, Body Fluids, and Being a Human Guinea Pig, by Jim Hogshire.** When an organ donor dies, more than a million dollars worth of medical procedures are set in motion. Doctors collect huge fees, hospitals rake in the dough, and lucky organ recipients get a new lease on life. *Everybody* profits from organ donation *except the donor.* But that's about to change. Jim Hogshire blows the lid off the body parts business. The author reveals exactly what your body is worth and how to sell it, in whole or in part. You can legally sell your blood, milk, sperm, hair, and other renewable resources — this book tells how. You can also make a living as a human guinea pig, renting your body to drug companies. It pays up to $100 a day, and this book lists over 150 test sites throughout the U.S.A. *1992, 5½ x 8, 164 pp, illustrated, soft cover. $7.95.*

☐ **64245 FREELANCE WRITER'S HANDBOOK, Second Edition, by James Wilson.** *Do you want to write? Why? Is it because you think it's an exciting career? Do you think it's glamorous, intellectual, emotionally rewarding, or perhaps, it pays well?* Much has happened since the first edition of this classic, and technological advancements have led to this second edition. New developments include faster computers, digital photography, e-mail, electronic submissions, and e-publishing, to name a few. Let a real professional show you the ropes. So before you quit your day job, check out **Freelance Writer's Handbook.** *2001, 5½ x 8½, 222 pp, soft cover. $15.95.*

☐ **64270 SATELLITE IMAGERY FOR THE MASSES, How to Use and Profit from the Satellite Revolution,** *by Harold Hough.* Once off limits to anyone but scientists, the technology of satellite interpretation is now available to anyone who can see its value on a business or personal basis. Thanks to the widespread availability of commercial satellite imagery, along with low prices and high quality images, opportunities for the average person who wants to break into this field are greater than ever before. Today satellite imagery is used in courts as legal evidence, by earth resources companies to find minerals, historians to better understand history, environmentalists to find pollution, and by civil engineers when choosing where to build infrastructures. The uses for this information are endless. The market for satellite imagery interpretation is wide open and holds potential rewards for those willing to explore the prospects, this book will give you the methods to get started. *2004, 5½ x 8½, 200 pp, illustrated, soft cover.* **$20.00.**

☐ **88888, LOOMPANICS UNLIMITED MAIN CATALOG,** See the catalog description on the last page of this book. *A complete catalog is sent* **FREE** *with every book order. If you would like to order the catalog separately it is* **5.00.**

**We offer the very finest in controversial and unusual books.**

**Check out our web site at
www.loompanics.com**

**Please send me the titles I have checked below.**

- ☐ 64266, Deep Inside the Underground Economy, $24.95
- ☐ 13077, How to Make Cash Money Selling at Swap Meets, Flea Markets, Etc., $12.95
- ☐ 64145, Shadow Merchants, $12.95
- ☐ 64167, Second-Hand Success, $14.95
- ☐ 14099, The Art & Science of Dumpster Diving, $14.95
- ☐ 64210 The Temp Worker's Guide to Self-Fulfillment, $12.95
- ☐ 64240 Make $$$ As A Non-Fiction Writer, $14.95
- ☐ 64267 Jobs Your Mother Never Wanted You To Have, $8.95
- ☐ 64129 Sell Yourself to Science, $7.95
- ☐ 64245, Freelance Writer's Handbook, $15.95
- ☐ 64270 Satellite Imagery For the Masses, $20.00
- ☐ 88888 Loompanics Unlimited Main Catalog, $5.00

UTT5

**LOOMPANICS UNLIMITED**
**PO BOX 1197**
**PORT TOWNSEND, WA 98368**

Please send me the books I have checked above. I am enclosing $ _____ which includes $6.25 for shipping and handling of orders up to $25.00. Add $1.00 for each additional $25.00 ordered. *Washington residents please include 8.3% for sales tax.*

**NAME** _____

**ADDRESS** _____

**CITY** _____

**STATE/ZIP** _____

We accept Visa, Discover, MasterCard, & American Express. To place a credit card order *only,* call 1-800-380-2230, 24 hours a day, 7 days a week.
Check out our web site: **www.loompanics.com**

# The Best Book Catalog In The World!!

We offer hard-to-find books on the world's most unusual subjects. Here are a few of the topics covered IN DEPTH in our exciting new catalog:

*Hiding/Concealment of physical objects!* A complete selection of the best books ever written on hiding things.

*Fake ID/Alternate Identities!* The most comprehensive selection of books on this little-known subject ever offered for sale! You have to see it to believe it!

*Investigative/Undercover methods and techniques!* Professional secrets known only to a few, now revealed to you to use! Actual police manuals on shadowing and surveillance!

*And much, much, more,* including Locks and Lock Picking, Self-Defense, Intelligence Increase, Money-Making Opportunities, Underground Economy, Exotic Weapons, Sex, Drugs, Anarchism, and more!

Our book catalog is over 230 pages, 8½ x 11, packed with more than 700 of the most controversial and unusual books ever printed! You can order every book listed! Periodic supplements keep you posted on the LATEST titles available!!! Our catalog is **$5.00**, including shipping and handling.

Our book catalog is truly THE BEST BOOK CATALOG IN THE WORLD! Order yours today. You will be very pleased, we know.

**LOOMPANICS UNLIMITED**
**PO BOX 1197**
**PORT TOWNSEND, WA 98368**

Name_____

Address _____

City/State/Zip _____

We accept Visa, Discover, American Express, and MasterCard.
For credit card orders *only*,
call **1-800-380-2330**, 24 hours a day, 7 days a week.
**Check out our Web site: www.loompanics.com**